THE LEGACY NAVIGATOR

CREATING INTENTIONAL MULTI-GENERATIONAL IMPACT

LANCE E. WELCH

burning soul press

The Legacy Navigator

Creating Intentional Multi-Generational Impact

Copyright © Lance E. Welch 2024

Cover Photo Credit: Dee Dee Designs

Photos of Author Credit: Joaquin Films Co.

ISBNs:

Hardcover: 978-1-950476-80-0

Paperback: 978-1-950476-78-7

eBook: 978-1-950476-79-4

PRAISE FOR THE LEGACY NAVIGATOR

"What an incredible read "The Legacy Navigator" is. As a fellow father and husband, this is the playbook that I wish I'd had sooner in my own life, filled with stories to help you grasp the concepts and also plan ahead, no matter where you are today. This book is going to change a lot of lives, whether you have kids yet or not, or are just looking for ways to get your financial situation more bulletproof and plan ahead for your own legacy.

Lance has a great ability to teach you the fundamentals on how to actually do all that, and along the way, a little bit of insight into the life and stories that he shares."

Brian A. Covey
Speaker, Author, EVP, Revolution Mortgage &
Founder, Covey Holdings, LLC.

"The fact that you're going to read about legacy says a lot about you. It says you know how fleeting life is and what truly matters over time is often overshadowed by things that won't. That's why you need to read Lance's book. It will help you leave a legacy that the people you love deserve."

Jeff Henderson
Author of *What to do Next*

"My first thought after reading "The Legacy Navigator" was "EVERYONE NEEDS TO READ THIS BOOK!" My friend has masterfully explored the profound impact of family bonds and how this impact can be extended generationally. This rediscovery of legacy serves as a personal reminder of the significance of connections, resilience, and the lasting influence we impart to those we love. Lance will take you on a beautiful journey that will stir your soul and remind you of the legacy you're shaping for your own family."

Dustin Smith
Author, Speaker, Artist, Pastor

"Within the pages of this insightful book, Lance delivers a profound message on intentional parenting and legacy building. His expertise shines as he guides readers through the transformative journey of raising children with purpose, not just for the present, but for generations to come. Through compelling real-life stories and practical examples, Lance skillfully demonstrates the importance of intentionality, emphasizing that true legacy encompasses more than mere finances.

With clear, step-by-step instructions, he equips readers to accelerate the fruits of a lifetime's labor, ensuring a lasting impact on future generations. A must-read for anyone seeking to create a meaningful legacy for their children and grandchildren."

Aaron Sanders
COO, Avoda Holdings, LLC.

"I've had the privilege of spending many hours with Lance Welch. Having read this book, I can honestly say that Lance isn't just writing about the topics and concepts discussed in these chapters... he's lived them. He's put these pages into practice in his own life, family and career. To me, that makes this book even more valuable, because it isn't just another how-to manual. It's a heartfelt challenge to make your life count.

As Lance says, none of us will accidentally create legacy. We have to be intentional about it, and this book is the perfect starting point for anyone ready to begin building their own."

Jeremy Weedman
Owner & Founder, AITod.ai

""The Legacy Navigator" is a new approach to creating multi generational impact for your family.

As an eleven year Navy veteran, I know that navigation floats between art and science as outside conditions create the need for adjusting your sails and course to reach your intended destination. You can plan for everything, and still not achieve your objective if you are not capable of changing along the way.

Written like a conversation between two friends, Lance lays out why it's important to empower future generations to continue to create wealth for the family according to the vision, values and knowledge you pass to them.

This book gives you tactical ideas and checklists, so your family is well-prepared for the future."

Chris Robinette
Founder, The Chris Robinette Company

"Lance has nailed it with "The Legacy Navigator". As a first time author, this will not be his last book. His clear and strong approach will help you become a Legacy Navigator. Like a great glass of brandy or bourbon, this book is strong and smooth at the same time. Men will be empowered to lead their families, women will appreciate the crystal clear approach to legacy, and the whole family will benefit from the thought-provoking questions at the end of each chapter. Thank you, Lance, for pouring your whole self and family into this incredible book."

Lisa Enebeli
Author, Speaker

"Lance Welch has used his personal and professional experience to lay the foundation for teaching others how to live a meaningful life through the transfer of legacy. I believe he has captured the heart of our current culture and provided a framework that enables families to intentionally prepare and transfer legacy. I recommend this book to those who are sincere in their desire to lead future generations well."

Stephanie Winslow
Author, Speaker, Legacy Coach

"If you have children—young or grown, or have a desire to have children one day—this book is for you! Lance, aka PopBear, has a unique gift to inspire, give practical wisdom on generational consciousness, and provide tools to create a legacy that will last. This book is a treasure that will add to your life and get passed down for generations."

Lindsey Welch
Entrepreneur

"Legacy planning is usually centered around wealth distribution and who is going to get what when. Lance has masterfully laid out a fresh way to think about what "intentional legacy" means through the "4 Legs of the Legacy Table" with a playbook on how to implement. If you want to protect your family's holistic legacy for 3,4, 5 generations to come - this is a must-read!"

Bijal Patel
Founder & CEO of LAUNCH, Speaker, award-winning Entrepreneur

""The Legacy Navigator" is a revelatory read that reshapes the way we think about creating lasting impacts for ourselves and our families. As a single mother of two, I found the book's guidance both practical and achievable, inspiring me to take meaningful action now rather than waiting until it's too late. It goes beyond mere financial inheritance, delving into the everyday choices that define our legacy. This book is a thought-provoking guide on living a life that truly matters."

Lauren Eckhardt
Best-selling & award winning Author, Ghostwriter, CEO of Burning Soul Press

DEDICATION

While writing this book, we had a very close friend pass away much too young. She was one of the finest persons you'd ever meet. Her capacity to love Jesus, her husband, her children, her grandchildren, her friends, and honestly people in general seemed limitless.

Her legacy of loving people and leaving them better off than before she met them is as strong and impactful as anyone you could ever know. She left just a little bit of herself with everyone she met.

It is a great honor that I get to call her friend for over 20 years and dedicate this book to Cindi Streitmatter...along with honoring her husband, Steve and their three grown children: Paige, Taylor, and Morgan. Thank you for sharing her with the world! She definitely made a positive impact!

This is also dedicated to my family – especially my wife, Allison, and three sons, Taylor, Logan, and Payton, from whom many of the experiences, lessons, and stories within these pages originated. The real gift of my legacy begins with each of you. You are truly my inspiration.

Finally, to my parents who literally had the deck stacked against them from the very beginning. In spite of that, their dedication to family and their marriage of nearly 60 years is truly an amazing legacy.

FOREWORD

TAYLOR A. WELCH

My dad is the greatest person that I know. I mean that sincerely. Not just because he wrote a book, a really good book, and I'm writing the foreword. That's all true. No, I believe that he's at the top of a very short list of people that I can truly trust. He's willing to be honest and ethical, and to share with me the tough stuff, the things that most people won't share with you because they're afraid to hurt your feelings or they're too opportunistic to call out your blind spots.

I remember as a kid growing up, I thought my dad knew everything and could do everything. And then you go through stages. One of those stages was when I began to feel like *I* knew everything and *I* could do everything. My dad patiently allowed me to make my own choices and offered to help. Most of the time, that looked like offering to help me pick up the pieces after I had blown something or messed something up.

One season in particular, we set up weekly meetings at a local Starbucks cafe where we would sit and he would teach me a variety of things. We would talk about goal setting, vision, and possibilities. And I learned in that season that my dad didn't just happen to know the things that he knew. It wasn't effortless. He didn't get lucky. He didn't inherit some fatherly level of smarts or wisdom. My dad went to leadership events. He read books. He hired coaches. He actually worked really hard to learn the things he was now teaching me.

We weren't rich at the time, but we were rich comparatively speaking. I say we weren't rich at the time because looking back, I am personally far better off now financially than we were back then. And I realize now that our level of living was healthy but modest. We were very rich in the areas that are far more important, though.

When you look at my dad now and you see his history of financial success, my dad has made it all and lost it all and made it all again. He has demonstrated that nothing in his life came down to luck. Everything came down to a purpose. And as I look back, I realized that my dad instilled a richness in me that I have now carried on into my family. Because of my dad's intentional focus on investing in his sons, we are rich in moments. We are rich in trust. We are rich in direction. We are rich in gratitude. We are rich in relationships.

Now, as a husband and father myself, we have everything that we need. And more than that, we have most of the things that we want as well. I attribute a lot of this to that season of my life when my dad would drag me out of bed and take me to a coffee shop to intentionally download into me. We would talk about topics such as, "Who are you becoming?", "What's the purpose of your life?", "What is your mission?", "Trust me, you don't want an hourly wage job." He taught me the value of asking great questions.

He would say, "One day you will have kids of your own and you will do this with them." Of course at the time, I was like, "whatever." But now I have an amazing son and a beautiful daughter of my own. And the greatest gift that I can think of growing up are those moments with my dad. When he showed me that no, he wasn't infallible. No, he was not perfect. But he WAS intentional – very intentional.

When you are intentional, you have certainty of direction. You don't have to move a hundred miles all at once. But a couple hundred feet a day in the right direction goes a long way. I think this book will give you a small dose of what I was blessed enough to experience growing up. I largely credit him for the businesses I own, the people that I've mentored, and ultimately the family that I get to lead today. My dad's legacy is certainly a tribute to being intentional with all four different legs of the legacy table, which you'll read about later.

If you're reading this, Dad, don't get too big of a head. Love you!

CONTENTS

INTRODUCTION

"Through a lens of navigation, then, we can see that "keeping" isn't about having a perfect, linear or flawless journey; keeping is about having a focus point that you want to keep moving toward."

– Benjamin L. Corey

Why is this called The Legacy Navigator? Navigation, or charting a course, is part art, part science, and part feel. It is having the urge to reach a desired location at some point in the future. While the concept of navigation is traditionally associated with ships and planes, it can also be easily applied to reaching your own ideal legacy. Both are focused on a desired end destination at some point in the future. For the navigator to be effective, he or she must first assess where they currently are, have at least a general idea of where they would like to end up (the clearer the better), AND have access to the tools and resources available for them to improve their likelihood of success.

For years, I worked with families to help chart a course of action to create an intentional legacy from purely a financial perspective. Some of these families are considered to be of high-net-worth: millionaires and multi-millionaires. Others, not so much. Regardless of your net worth, creating an intentional legacy is ultimately about setting up your family for a greater future than what was provided for you in the following areas: relational, financial, spiritual, emotional, and physical. I'm not yet a multi-millionaire, but one of my sons is and my other sons will be! Not that money is how I measure success, because it's not. However, the lessons and importance of familial relationships which we instilled in them when they were younger have served them quite well.

To be honest, most of the high-net-worth families I worked with were only concerned about the financial side of their family legacy. When that's the only focus, statistics say their wealth will be gone within two or three generations. I'll share more on that a little later.

I have three sons and I was shaping the direction of their future well before they could ever comprehend what I was doing. I was dead-set on them having a better future than anything I had ever experienced at the time. That's not to say I did everything right. Actually, I was far from it. BUT my wife and I were incredibly intentional about doing all we could to set the trajectory of their lives to be far more successful than we were.

And they are proving that all of our inconveniences were worth it. Even at their current young ages, their wisdom and confidence in knowing who they are far surpasses what we knew at their same ages. Does this mean that they consistently make choices that I'm thrilled about? Heavens, no! BUT they are making choices out of an identity of knowing who they are and that no matter what, they are deeply loved, will always have a seat available to them around our table, and are fully accepted as a Welch. No matter what!

This book will challenge your thoughts on the meaning of legacy, help you ask the right questions to assess where you currently are, and it will resource you with thoughts and phrases to create a vision for what you would truly like your legacy to be. Finally, it will provide actual examples of what we did that worked well and some exercises for you to implement with your own family to greatly improve the likelihood of setting up your heirs for amazing success.

I believe that when your focus is to be intentional to set up future generations to be more successful than you were, to give them the ability to think for themselves, to create healthy pride in the family name (identity), and to give them the tools and resources to equip them to go to the next level, you will have found the recipe to creating a family legacy that will stand the test of time!

1

A LEGACY BASELINE

"Live your life in such a way that you'll be remembered for your kindness, compassion, fairness, character, benevolence, and a force for good who had much respect for life, in general."

– Germany Kent

A LEGACY WILL BE BESTOWED on us all, whether we are intentional about the legacy we leave at our passing or not. A legacy is no respecter of persons, net worth, ethnicity, gender, socio-economic status, or any other measurement. You really only have two options: you can settle for the default legacy or you can have an intentional one. The question isn't, "Will I leave a legacy to and for my family?" but rather, "Which legacy will I be leaving?" Let's level-set right here – nice and early in our journey together. Leaving a legacy is much, much more than a financial inheritance. While a financial inheritance may be a key component and possibly even your top priority, it's actually only about a quarter of the full picture. I'll expound on that shortly!

For starters, let's look at your calendar. It will highlight areas getting your intentional focus. Your calendar will shine a light into what or whom you are truly intentionally investing your time. Your current disciplines, priorities, and passions will dictate the type of legacy you will leave at your passing, as well as the length of time during which you'll have generational impact and influence. Your intentionality and execution will give insight into how many generations your legacy will influence, particularly with your heirs, but also society as a whole.

I've had some people argue that even though their family is not placed anywhere on their calendar, it does not mean their family isn't important. And this is true. I fully agree with that. But when something is important AND intentional, in my experience, it will be written down somewhere and that location is usually their calendar. Disciplines, priorities, and passions will always surface and it is crystal clear as to their importance. You, my friend, ARE leaving a legacy whether you plan on it or not. Recognizing this to be true, it's time to level up your intentionality and this book will help direct your steps.

It's like when someone passes away "intestate", which means without a formal last will and testament. In this case, the state will have one created for you. They (the state) will determine what they deem to be the best way to share your assets and process your estate. And in the event that you have children who are minors, the state will take it upon themselves to determine who is best suited to assume their guardianship! Do you really trust a governmental entity to create something that aligns with your personal wishes? Probably not. I define this type of legacy as the default legacy because it is simply created by default. It is always easy to assume you have already laid out your baseline wishes in your last will and testament. But there is a surprising percentage of families without even a basic will. So, I strongly encourage you to start there.

The default legacy lacks focus, specificity, and intentionality towards a clear and beneficial outcome for the next generation. The end result? They end up leaving a legacy they didn't intend on leaving. Granted, there may be some people who really do *not* care about how they're remembered after they are gone, nor do they care that their heirs are taken care of. However, I am virtually 100% certain they are not the ones likely to pick up a book like this, let alone read it.

Consider this: What are the chances that, even though I'm aware of what it takes to create a specific legacy but choose to keep pushing it to the back burner, that I will somehow, miraculously, leave a legacy that is exactly what I would have wanted for my family? I'd say somewhere between slim and none. But here's one of the wonderful side benefits of leaving an intentional legacy: as I'm intentionally building my ideal legacy, I'm getting to enjoy it with my heirs along the way. Obviously, once I'm gone, I will have no ability to see how my kids, grandkids, or great-grandkids are enjoying my legacy efforts. Still, I will know that I did everything within my power to set up future generations for even greater success than I had.

In the mid '90's, I remember briefly working with a family who was worth approximately $150 million at that time. The three kids, the future heirs, invited me to visit with their father about working with a team of specialists to create a plan which would drastically reduce or offset their looming estate tax bill. At that time, the top estate tax bracket was 50% for estates over $5 million. With just some simple math, you can see that the government was set to become the largest single benefactor of this estate. Unfortunately, dear ole dad had no interest in reducing his future tax bill and helping out his heirs. I still remember his response: "I started out with nothing, less than nothing actually. Even after taxes they are gonna be millions of dollars ahead of where I started. So I really don't feel too sorry for them." Meeting over! Needless to say, there wasn't a strong sense of unity within this family.

Some may see this as a group of young adults with an entitlement mentality because they were upset with their dad for not taking the estate tax situation seriously and "costing" them millions of dollars in taxes. However, they really did have a valid concern. The vast majority of the estate was physical real estate, inventory, a business valuation that would be based on an IRS formula, and a relatively small amount of their assets were liquid. They actually had very little cash with which to pay the estate tax bill. Even though the patriarch had successfully built a strong financial foundation for his family, the likely legacy was one tainted with negative undertones because there was no real communication within the family unit. This was a legacy built solely on a financial inheritance.

Finances are only one part of a healthy legacy. In fact, it's only one of the four areas of focus as this book explores creating an intentional legacy. My wife has constantly said, "We will always make room around our table for our sons and their families to feel welcomed." So, from that mental framework, I will be sharing about the four legs of the legacy table.

The intentional legacy, in its most simplistic form, will leverage a variety of documents that make sure your wishes, financial and otherwise, are identified, communicated, and executed so they are lived out in a clear, concise, and structured manner. This will require those creating the intentional legacy to have intimate knowledge of all the various types of assets, intellectual property, family philosophies, and values. It will also possibly include a statement of faith, as well as their view on generosity and philanthropic ventures.

In my experience, more effort and intentional planning is put into planning a wedding or a vacation than even just the financial portion of the estate or the distribution of assets. Study after study shows that creating wealth is statistically easier than making sure it is perpetuated beyond the next couple of generations. If you're reading this, there's a solid chance that you have a multi-generational awareness about you. You may also hear it described as having a generational consciousness. I'd even be willing to bet you've already given some thought about what your legacy could or should look like.

There are many definitions of a legacy. One definition that has stuck with me over the years is one I heard at a wealth conference I attended many years ago: *One's legacy is that thing that refuses to be buried when they are.* While this may be true, it does nothing to explain the power and relative ease of being intentional with your legacy. Being intentional about creating the type of legacy you want to outlive your time on this earth is not rocket science. For many people, all they need is a little encouragement in the form of recommended next steps, legacy resources, and just a little bit of accountability. Anything unclear or confusing will tend to be seen as far more difficult than it really is and will typically be delayed so long that it's eventually left undone altogether.

For much of my career, I was in the financial services industry. A good portion of those years were spent specifically working with various advisors of high-net-worth families with potential estate tax liabilities to structure effective and efficient wealth transfer vehicles. I honestly do not recall even one conversation about what it would take to increase the likelihood of all their wealth extending into perpetuity. Call it naïve but at the time, I thought all that was needed was to make sure the right legal documents were in place to prevent the government from being one of the biggest heirs to a family's wealth. Unfortunately, none of the parties involved, not the families nor their advisors, ever discussed the very high likelihood of their family assets being virtually gone within three generations. I'll share some statistics on this shortly.

During those times of working with the wealthy family and their advisory team, it wasn't uncommon that the heirs were never brought in during the decision-making process until it was almost finished and their signatures were needed. The heirs were often left in the dark as to what all went into the planning process, the reason certain trusts were being used, how this planning would benefit them, or how the planning could greatly restrict their access to a full and immediate inheritance upon the death of the family's patriarch or matriarch. When the heirs were conspicuously left out of the entire planning process, it tended to create an "us versus them" paradigm. The best way to create a multi-generational culture is getting as much buy-in and alignment as possible *before* all documents are ready to be executed.

It was important to everyone that taxes didn't negate their decades of wealth accumulation efforts. Still, on more than one occasion I heard this phrase: "I really just hope all of our [financial] success doesn't screw up our kids." At the time, I had young kids but I did *not* have the life experience to comprehend where they came from. Fast forward over 25 years later, and now I get it. I totally get it. I've seen plenty of examples of how creating an easy life for one's children proved to be quite detrimental to them in their future.

> **Creating an easy life for your kids robs them of building the inner strength necessary to persevere when tough times come knocking on their door.**

And tough times will come – they always come. Knowing this to be true, it makes sense to prepare your kids, even your adult kids, to handle the good and the not-so-good. Whether you have a vast amount of wealth or only a little, this book is designed to share some wealth transfer statistics as well as simple, easy-to-implement steps for creating a legacy of your own choosing. However, just because I claim these steps are simple and easy, it does *not* mean it will be automatic. As Jim Rohn used to say, "What's easy to do, is also easy not to do."

Doing anything worthwhile will be inconvenient. At a leadership event I attended, I heard author and speaker John Maxwell say, "Everything worthwhile is uphill. People have uphill hopes and they have downhill habits." Unfortunately, most people aren't willing to be inconvenienced in the moment! It will be inconvenient to be intentional about leaving a specific legacy. It will be inconvenient setting up the necessary legal documents to mitigate taxes. It will be inconvenient to pass along the intangibles of your legacy. Saying yes to leaving the desired legacy will mean saying no to some other things. Saying yes to anything has a cost associated with it. Sticking your head in the sand is the most costly option available.

Inconvenience is honestly just a normal part of life. The interesting thing is that you get to choose your inconvenience. It will be inconvenient to put the time, energy, effort, and resources into creating an intentional legacy. If you choose not to be inconvenienced right now with all of the planning pieces, you will still be faced with a much larger inconvenience when things regarding your legacy end up going south. An inconvenience doesn't have to be seen as a negative. Your inconvenience can have a positive return tied to it. So, choose your inconvenience.

For those choosing *not* to leave an intentional legacy, it will most certainly prove an even greater inconvenience later when you realize your lack of intentionality (and lack of follow-through) resulted in entitled children, leading to weak adults, and eventually a dwindling estate! There's inconvenience in planning out your ideal legacy, or there's inconvenience in settling for the default legacy and your family name ends up penniless within three generations. Choose your inconvenience.

In talking about your legacy baseline, there are two points to consider. First, assume your legacy starts right now and *no* additional planning or legal docs are in place than what already exists. Does it create the legacy of your choosing? Next, determine with absolute certainty what your minimally acceptable legacy could be. Vow to begin *now* to get with those that can help you stack the deck in your favor to create your ideal legacy!

Disclaimer: You may literally do everything right and have things still not turn out the way you had pictured. Planning is not an insurance policy that guarantees your kids will get a solid grasp of everything you're teaching and that they will be able to effectively implement these teachings when they get older. These steps, however, will stack the deck for them and all future generations!

CHAPTER APPLICATION

Reflection:

- You *will* leave a legacy upon your departure from this earth.
- For your legacy, you can choose between the default version or the intentional version.
- Not all inconveniences are negative. Framed and viewed correctly, they can have a positive return associated with them. Choose your inconvenience.
- It is important to make sure estate taxes do not take up most of your financial estate at death, but this is not the biggest consideration when creating an intentional legacy.

Implementation:

- Take a few minutes to think about how your legacy looks as it is right now.
- Take a few minutes to think about how your legacy could look.
- Write down your thoughts from above. This can be short and sweet – two to four sentences. This is *not* where you'll get down into the weeds...keep it simple for now.

2

INTENTIONAL LEGACY

"I think of life as a good book. The further you get into it, the more it begins to make sense."

– Harold S. Kushner

CREATING TRUE MULTI-GENERATIONAL IMPACT is not a "pie in the sky" pipe dream. There are tried-and-true, tested and vetted processes that many families have used for generations to create a legacy that they and their heirs are proud of. They were intentional, not perfect. There is a precursor to being intentional, and that is being aware of what you desire. Logically, you really can't claim to be intentional and not be able to define what you are being intentional about. So yes, it stands to reason that if you plan to take intentional actions toward something desired, you will first put in at least a little effort to know what you would like to be intentional about.

Let me share a story on what made me realize the level of intentionality some families had taken to create a legacy for their family name. A good number of years into my financial services career, I had earned a payoff trip to a quaint little area on the east coast near Providence, Rhode Island. One evening, we had a private reception and dinner at someone's personal residence. This place just happened to be around forty thousand square feet! It sat on approximately six acres with a backyard that had a gentle slope down to the Atlantic Ocean. It was absolutely gorgeous. We were given a private tour of the property and we learned that the family was quite wealthy, obviously, and that this particular property had been in the family for four generations.

We also learned that the family only used the property for themselves for four to five weeks out of the year. Nevertheless, they had a year-round staff of twenty-seven people that kept up with the grounds and the interior of the property for both informal and formal events. When the family wasn't personally using the property, it was used only sporadically throughout the year for special events and tours.

During the four to five weeks when the family was onsite, they brought in the various heads of their different companies for an annual review and projections meeting. It is important to note that the heads of their companies were all family members. Those executives also brought their adult children to sit in on those meetings to personally witness the review and projections process. By including the younger generation, they were being conditioned early and often on how to do a particular task, think through various challenges and opportunities, and continue to grow the family's net worth and influence.

By the time the younger generation was preparing to take over for their aging parents, they had amassed decades of experience with on-the-job training and strategic thinking. This is *the* process that creates generational legacy. It's not rocket science, but it is obviously highly effective. It could potentially even be seen as painfully boring and time-consuming to the younger generation. Still, it's a tried-and-true method of perpetuating wealth from generation to generation.

This intentional, methodical, time-consuming process is what allows for all aspects of one's legacy to create impact in perpetuity. Perpetuating wealth isn't as easy as one might think. In fact, it's rather uncommon for wealth to be sustained beyond those who created it.

Statistically speaking, the Williams Group wealth consultancy found that *70% of the families who inherited vast wealth will lose it by the end of the second generation and 90% by the end of the third*.

This statistic should be a wake-up call that simply having wealth isn't enough to ensure it lasts from one generation to the next. You will never be able to address a problem if you're unaware of it. Let these percentages sink in and motivate you to become highly intentional. What differentiates those families with generational wealth from those without is that the kids have decades of experience. They don't just simply inherit wealth; they are taught how to maintain and even create it.

These percentages support the adage, *"shirtsleeves to shirtsleeves in three generations"*. In simple terms, this is the concept that future generations have problems hanging on to wealth. Therefore, it was up to the generation that created the wealth to roll their shirt sleeves up and get to work. For many, wealth passes on to the second generation that did not have to work hard for it so they couldn't fully appreciate it nor understand what it took to create it.

Since this second generation never acquired the skill set to create wealth, they were weak in maintaining it and certainly had no ability to train the third generation. As such, they have very little in the way of knowledge to teach the third generation anything about wealth creation or preservation. This means the third generation departs this earth with little to *no* wealth. Now if familial wealth is to be created, the next generation will have to roll up their shirt sleeves and make it happen on their own, just like their great-grandparents did.

For those families that got lumped into the "shirtsleeves to shirtsleeves" statistic, there was one thing that almost all of them had in common: they didn't have the life experience and discipline to create wealth in the same industry into which they were now stepping. They were simply inheriting wealth. Without this specialized knowledge and experience, the wealth begins to dissipate through undisciplined spending.

By the third generation, they typically end up back to where their great-grandparents were prior to their wealth creation. Now, the next generation must roll up their shirt sleeves and get to work. This is where we get the phrase, *"shirtsleeves to shirtsleeves in three generations"*. The answer to this dilemma is not more legal documents to restrict your heirs' access to the wealth. Having a generational consciousness starts with determining what is most important to you *and* becoming intentional about making sure future generations have a solid understanding of the philosophies and habits for creating and maintaining wealth.

In creating wealth, the patriarch or matriarch had thirty, forty, even fifty years or more to learn how to create and maintain wealth. All too often, they fear losing control and also loath inefficiencies so they typically fail to "train up" the next generation. Thus, when a death occurs, the heirs often have less than a year to figure out what took the previous generation decades to master. One might think handling lots of money can't be all that hard. Handling it isn't the problem – it's making it last for multiple generations.

A common pattern over the last couple of decades, unfortunately, is that the elders are choosing to not divulge the depths of their wealth with their heirs. The reasons for this vary from not wanting their heirs to begin asking for handouts, to feeling as if they are doing their children a favor by making them earn their own way, to the patriarchs' desire to maintain complete control for as long as possible. All these reasons and more contribute to the heirs' lack of experience in dealing with large amounts of wealth and the strategic thinking required to continue growing the family's net worth.

To further exacerbate this problem, many planners and advisors strive to set up financial and legal documents to "protect" future generations from themselves. I witnessed plans that gave a percentage of the family wealth at certain ages; or a specific percentage or lump sum upon graduation; or a bonus amount for an advanced degree; or "X" amount when they got married. Sometimes funds were withheld if they didn't finish college or if they got into trouble with the law. There is virtually no shortage of ways to restrict an heir's access to wealth.

What message does this send to the heirs? To me, it implies the belief that future generations won't have the discipline or expertise to create and manage wealth without guidelines. Some from the younger generation told me it implied to them that they were not smart enough to hang on to it, let alone increase it for future generations.

What traditionally happens when someone is told they can't have something or that they aren't good enough for it? It usually makes them start looking for creative ways to get to it anyway. And now they are more focused on successfully obtaining it than on maximizing wealth for themselves, representing the family name, or positively impacting future generations.

Some will rebel and do all they can to bypass the rules. Others cower with rejection and accept the verdict that implies they are "less than" and continue to live in a manner that validates this given persona. Neither of these scenarios are what I would consider healthy. Rest assured, there is a better way, but it will be inconvenient. It will cost you. Everything worthwhile has a cost, but there is also an expected return.

Herein lies the premise behind this book's mission to navigate the creation of an amazing legacy.

Future generations are just as capable, likely more so, than previous generations and can successfully grow the family net worth *when* there is intentionality to do more than just set up wealth transfer vehicles.

When you are intentional about transferring your family's values, vision, and knowledge, and not just your wealth alone, you can create a sequence of events that will pull your family name out of the massive pile of mediocrity and avoid being a part of the previously aforementioned statistics!

In other words, done correctly, you can perpetuate your family name and defy the odds of the "*shirtsleeves to shirtsleeves in three generations*" curse. The things you stood for and fought for will be immortalized instead of simply passing wealth to the next generation. Wealth transfer vehicles are an absolute necessity, but it's these "soft" traits that are most often overlooked. I'm going to equip you with some tools and the necessary mindset which will help you empower your heirs to promote wealth longevity.

Many families who are intentional about gathering around the family dinner table, whether for meals or games, claim a much stronger familial connection than those who don't. This tradition allows for growth and understanding of those around you. Consistent proximity to a specific group of people is an intentional act as well as a priority of your conscious will. One is not too busy for something they deem a significant priority. Camaraderie, trust, education, and training will all come from proximity. For generationally conscious minded people, spending intentional time around the table is honestly one of the easiest tools at your disposal as you begin embedding your legacy into the future generation.

If you want a starting point, I created an assessment tool to come alongside this book as another resource to help you gauge how much progress you have already made towards your intentional legacy. In two and a half minutes, it will shine a light on some specific areas that warrant additional attention. Once you are aware of where you are in this legacy journey, you can now make intentional, calculated decisions on which areas you will focus on next. The assessment aligns perfectly with the contents of this book. Access it for free at www.legacyreadiness.com.

Let's dig into the **Four Legs of the Legacy Table.** Surprisingly, I get a decent amount of pushback when I start talking about spending family time around a dinner table. I remember the days when all three of my boys were in the same sport, during the same time of year, and occasionally would all have games on the exact same night on three different fields! So yes, I understand a nightly gathering around the dinner table can prove to be more the exception than the rule. Humor me and let's look deeper anyway, shall we?

As I mentioned previously, the wealthy families I worked with were often concerned that their wealth would possibly "screw up our kids." Children of wealthy families tend to have it a little easier, which can be a blessing but could also prove to be a detriment! An unfortunate pattern of wealth can look like the following:

An overly easy childhood can lead to entitled children; entitled children tend to lead to weak and undisciplined adults; weak, undisciplined adults lead to them burning through their wealth at a pace where they pass away broke, leaving nothing for future generations.

Statistically, this is a *fact.* Obviously, this is not the best recipe to make sure your financial legacy beats the statistics we discussed earlier.

Many that I worked with were almost exclusively focused on

setting up the right financial vehicles and employing the best legal documents to make sure the government didn't become one of their largest heirs. Unfortunately, getting the wealth *to* the next generation is not all that difficult; the challenge is making sure it's still available to transfer to the subsequent generations.

So, what are the four most consistent pieces of the puzzle? What do you need in your arsenal in order to leave an intentional legacy that can withstand being transferred from generation to generation? The things most imperative to creating a sustainable, multi-generational transfer are as follows:

1. Vision
2. Values
3. Knowledge
4. Wealth

When families have an intentional strategy for transferring their vision, values, and knowledge, the transfer of wealth becomes much more efficient and effective. When intentionally identifying and creating the legacy of your choice, there is almost a supernatural transference of that legacy to the two or three generations currently living on this planet. You cannot address something of which you aren't aware. With your cognizance piqued, you will then find yourself uniquely equipped to create *and* transfer the legacy that best represents who you are and what you stand for to your future heirs.

In my time working with those with wealth, we most often focused on the estate tax side of things. With proper planning, one can make sure that the government isn't the biggest benefactor of your hard work. In my opinion, the wealth transfer piece is honestly the easiest to address. This process highly leverages the expertise of others to understand the various financial and legal documents necessary to, at the very least, get the wealth TO the next generation. Still, absent of generational intentionality, it all but excuses the benefactors from truly under-standing the entirety of their plans due to the trust they place with their professional advisors.

The same cannot be said about the transfer of their vision, values, and knowledge. This requires an even higher level of personal involvement. Your attorney and financial advisor are not likely to create the means for the effective transfer of these other three legs of the table without your personal involvement. With that said, let's take a deeper look at all four legs.

CHAPTER APPLICATION

Reflection:

- There are tried, tested, and proven methods to create an intentional legacy.
- A legacy is more than a transfer of wealth. It's also the transfer of family vision, values, and knowledge.
- An easy childhood can lead to entitled children; entitled children often lead to weak and undisciplined adults; and weak, undisciplined adults lead to burning through family wealth.

Implementation:

- Begin to think of what you would like your family legacy to look like.
- Consider setting aside a special notebook or journal to begin writing down ideas of your ideal legacy that come to mind as you read through this book.

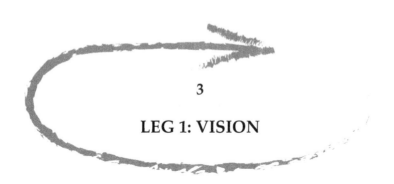

3

LEG 1: VISION

"The only thing worse than being blind is having sight but no vision."

– Helen Keller

IS IT POSSIBLE TO HAVE SIGHT and yet have no vision? Unfortunately, yes. I'm taking a little bit for granted here in assuming you understand the difference between sight and vision. To be honest, if you're like me, until I read this quote it didn't carry the same weight. We have often used those words interchangeably. Granted, deep down, we know the difference. So, in this context, we'll be focused on the concept of planning for the future.

In what I get to do–helping people level up their businesses, marriages, and family–I often get to work with very talented folks who haven't really thought about the importance of a family vision, let alone a vision for their legacy. Many are so busy creating a better standard of living for themselves and their families that they leave little time to create a family vision.

The Bible says, "Where there is no vision, the people perish"

(Proverbs 29:18a KJV). As this phrase pertains to your legacy, what this simply means is that without having clarity in your family legacy, it is very unlikely to turn out in a way that makes you proud. You may have a vague, back-burner picture of what you would like your legacy to look like, but without extreme clarity, the chances of the desired outcome becoming reality is very slim. Developing a clear vision for your family legacy will require the investment of your time and attention.

In a business leadership talk, John Maxwell described the creation of a corporate vision as three simple points:

- Vision starts within.
- Vision draws on your history.
- Vision meets the needs of others.

Since he was referring to corporate leadership, let's adjust that for our family or legacy vision discussion. What does it mean for a vision to start from within? First, this means it must be *yours*, not someone else's. It's ok to get ideas from other places, but for it to be effectively implemented and passed on to your other family members, it must be from within you! If you take a short cut by capturing someone else's vision for their legacy, I can all but promise you it will fail.

Vision starts within. Having a vision means that we gain a picture of a future that is bigger, brighter, and/or healthier than our present. There is a training that I have borrowed from my oldest son that he calls "Push vs. Pull" (I'm sure that came from me somehow, so I don't mind "borrowing" it back from him). With a Push vision, I'm constantly in a grind mode to "make" something happen; doing something someone else wants or expects me to do. With a Pull vision, my vision is so attractive, so enticing that I'm constantly energized every time I do something that I know is going to feed the vision and bring it into reality.

Vision draws on our history. There is a wonderfully

powerful phrase I picked up from the book, "The Gap and the Gain" authored by Dr. Benjamin Hardy and Dan Sullivan. In that book, they share a strategy they call AMB. This stands for "Always Measure Backwards." In measuring backwards, we allow ourselves to intentionally focus on the growth from where we were to where we are now. And my own little twist on AMB is when I envision a bigger, brighter, healthier future, I'm able to visualize backwards from that future point and implement actions and behaviors *now* that will support the desired end result. The late Steve Jobs said, "You can't connect the dots looking forward; you can only connect them looking backwards." And Soren Kierkegaard said, "Life can only be understood backwards; but must be lived forwards."

Vision meets the needs of others. A vision that only focuses on *me*, is arrogant at best and narcissistic (arrogance at the expense of others) at worst. Throughout our time together in this book, we'll continually focus on others, and specifically our heirs. In other words, we'll ask, "What can I do today to have a multi-generational impact on *my* family lineage?" When I am focused on the needs of others, there will almost always be a strong relational element tied to it. As a parent creating an intentional legacy, it really doesn't matter how old my kids or heirs are. The stronger the relationship, the greater the influence. Something I'm seeing in my relationships with my sons is that as long as my relationships with them are healthy, I have a greater level of influence without coming across like a dictator. Besides, open and honest conversations with my family teaches me more about strengthening our family legacy.

The challenge I most often hear about creating an intentional legacy is they don't know where to start. That's why you're reading this book. Within the chapters of this book, you will find multiple resources and exercises to greatly simplify the vision creation and implementation process.

You may or may not have come from a family that gave much

thought to vision, let alone a personal legacy. And to be honest, that's irrelevant at this moment. Whether you did or didn't, it's up to you to create your own vision for your family. While it may be a little easier for you to grasp the concepts of creating a vision for your legacy if you came from a family that cast vision while you were growing up. Grasping the concept and implementing the concept are two different things. So now, it's all in your court. The opportunity to build your vision starts today.

There's an axiom that postulates, "Wherever you look, that's as far as you can see." If you want to see further, you must position yourself further down the road. This is true in the physical world and it is most certainly true in the legacy planning world, too. The more you work on identifying the type of legacy you would like to see, the more you'll begin to recognize resources available to help you clarify what it could look like; what you feel it SHOULD look like. It's quite amazing, really. The clearer you get on what you want, the more resources are identified to help you get there. So, once you get an idea of what you would like to see, the more often you will come across additional ideas and resources to help you get where you want to go.

Similarly, the more you focus on what type of legacy you'd like to create, the more you'll see things in your day-to-day activities that provide insight into defining the vision for your family's legacy. You cannot intentionally improve anything without first having an idea of where you are and to what extent it could be improved. In other words, your heightened awareness of your current family legacy will begin to bring into focus what you would really like your legacy to be.

If you never give any thought to your own personal story and how it can impact your family's future generations, you'll live your life in service almost entirely to yourself. This may not bother you today, but in my experience, someday it will. Developing a vision is not a one-time activity. You don't sit down, brainstorm for a bit, come up with a vision for your family legacy and never give it another thought. No, that's not how it works. It doesn't work that way for your businesses, so why would it work that way for your personal vision? A "one and done" mentality doesn't work well in any area of planning. There are too many ever-changing variables for that mindset to work.

When our oldest was barely a teenager, we implemented the "Welch Family Vision Cast" at the end of each calendar year. The first year we did it, the vision cast was a simple one-pager with basic questions. I simply adapted the year-end business review I had created for my sales team that I called a "Reflect and Plan" into something I could use with my family. In Chapter 11, you will create and implement your own family vision cast.

Chapter Application

Reflection:

- You cannot delegate your family's vision to an objective third party.
- Without a vision of where you would like to end up, any path will get you to your destination.
- A heightened awareness of your current legacy could bring into focus just how amazing your legacy could be.

Implementation:

- Focus on the relational element of your vision. How can you strengthen your family relationships? What could that look like?
- Identify how your legacy looks today versus how you would like it to look.
- Define a legacy that acts as a Pull strategy and not a Push strategy.

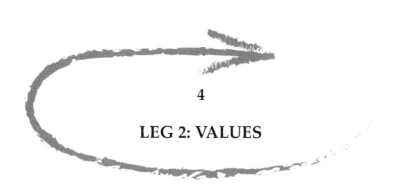

4

LEG 2: VALUES

"Your core values are the deeply held beliefs that authentically describe your soul."

– John C. Maxwell

ONE OF MY EARLY MENTORS used to say, "Your values are more effectively caught than taught." This is so, so true. I can be highly intentional in teaching my kids about my values, but they are significantly more likely to mirror my actions than "follow directions". The only thing louder than me *telling* my kids what's important is *showing* them. I've always kept this quote in the back of my mind: "Your actions speak so loudly, I cannot hear what you are saying," by Ralph Waldo Emerson.

As a parent, the question is not, *did my kids see how I reacted*? Rather, it's *what did they see*? As a parent, you are never *not* on the clock. When you're at home, your language, actions, responses, and behaviors are always on full display. The things your children see you do, even adult children, will be interpreted as the right way to do things...as well as the most important things to be done.

I remember a time when I had my oldest son in the car with me and we were going through a drive-through at a restaurant. He was probably around four years old. The attendant gave me back way too much change. Once I realized that, we returned to the restaurant, went inside together, and returned the excess change. Does my son remember that today? Probably not. But at his subconscious level, he has a foundational perspective that there is a right way to handle this particular situation...you return the excess change. He may not attribute this specific event as a core value from nearly 30 years ago, but an intentional decision was made on my part to model "do as I do, not just as I say."

There is a story of one quick-thinking mom who was taking her seven-year-old daughter to school one morning. Typically, the father took his daughter to school on his way to the office. But this particular morning, Mom was driving her to school.

When they were almost at the school, the seven-year-old little girl asked, "Hey Mom, where are all of the other stupid *!@!#! idiot drivers today?"

Without missing a beat, Mom said, "Oh don't worry dear, those drivers are only out on the roads when your father is driving." Obviously, the little girl was picking up on some choice words when dad was the one driving. It's the adage *monkey see, monkey do.*

Our kids are incredibly observant. They are like little sponges, soaking up the good, the bad, and the ugly. Knowing this to be true, how easy could it be to intentionally impart important messages and life lessons to your kids? Obviously, this requires you, Mom and Dad, to know what your values are. What do you stand for? What are the characteristics that matter the most to you? Are they written down and discussed as a family?

"Lessons are more effectively caught than taught." While I agree with that, much will still be lost if we only rely on "caught", because it lacks intentionality. Relying on lessons to be *caught* opens the door to a generational disconnect caused by faulty interpretation and assumptions. I know from experience that without the re-telling of stories from previous generations, the lessons and experiences are eventually lost. For those lessons that you'd like to run deep within your family lines, you must reiterate them often.

One such lesson I used to repeat to my boys, mainly as teenagers and young adults, was, "I am not here to be popular with you. I'm here to get you to the next level. But someday, I assure you, I will be quite popular with you." There were plenty of instances where I wasn't very popular with them. And I would remind them *why* I was ok not being "popular." They heard that phrase so much they would start saying it with me. Then it got to the point where I would catch a subtle eye-roll the moment I would start this phrase. But I was so incredibly intentional to prepare them for the next level that I was completely ok NOT being popular. And now, I have an amazing, mutually-respectful relationship with all three of my sons.

I call this intentionality, "future casting." As a parent, I feel it's my responsibility to model *and* communicate the values that really matter to me and that I want to see in their futures. As the patriarch, I am the point man (by the way, "Point Man" is an incredible book by Steve Farrar). It is my responsibility to know the way, go the way, and show the way. Arguably the most important of those three is the "show the way" part. To show the way requires me to make sure they understand what I'm doing and why it is important. Sometimes, oftentimes, it requires that I slow down and communicate my intentions. Sometimes it requires that I ask questions of the next generation to confirm understanding.

Granted, it is often inconvenient to slow down and ask questions. But it is an inconvenience that will pay huge dividends. This model of training is possibly decades long. It prepares your children to someday carry the mantle of the family name! The likelihood of the next generation being able to train *their* children is initiated well before they have children of their own. This one action may have one of the greatest impacts on securing a generational consciousness in the lives of your heirs.

Quick question: Do you know what the top five core values are for your family? If you don't, don't worry, you are not alone. Everyone has a very specific value system by which they operate. However, very few families have them identified, written down, and communicate them regularly within the family. For that very purpose, I've included a Core Value Exercise in Appendix A for you to complete. Feel free to put a bookmark in this page and jump to Appendix A now, before going any further.

The core value exercise is very simple but definitely not easy. I suggest you and your spouse or partner take the time to complete the exercise separately. See if your values overlap. I often see overlap but rarely see the *exact* same values chosen. Please know that is ok. Once you both have your own core five for a total of 10 values, work together to bring those 10 values down to the top five for the family as a unit. If you happen to be a single individual at the moment, please go ahead and complete this for yourself.

YOUR IDENTITY CREATES YOUR VALUES

"Storytelling is the greatest activity of any culture. Storytelling is how you build a family, how you pass along identity."

– Randall Wallace

The identity of a family is probably the most contagious aspect of what I teach. Identity is rarely formally taught. And yet, it is arguably the most easily transferable characteristic of anything we'll discuss because the younger generation simply emulates the older generation. Identity is definitely more caught.

So, which comes first: doing or being? Where should you focus your attention? Should you begin by focusing on what you would like to teach your heirs? Or should you become hypersensitive to who you are and what you stand for? Everything starts and ends with one's identity. It could be said that one can have clearly articulated values without ever working on their identity. Yes, technically, that can be true. But it's still one's identity that shapes their values. Show me someone with very high, altruistic, philanthropic values and we'll be able to tie those values intimately to their identity. Further, that same person will tend to pass on those same values to their heirs.

Said another way, it's possible to come up with some very decisive values that would make anyone proud. But if one's identity isn't aligned with their values, those clearly defined values will be short-lived. The old saying of "fake it 'til you make it" can only last for so long! Can one change his or her identity? Absolutely. And this isn't just my opinion. With intentionality, a clearly defined, targeted outcome, and a solid support structure, one's identity can most definitely be shifted. This has been widely studied and validated. For an additional resource, check out "Personality Isn't Permanent" by Dr. Benjamin Hardy.

Just like a family legacy, your family's identity will either be created on purpose or by default. In fact, your legacy and identity are intimately intertwined. With the default option, you are completely winging it. The percentages are quite high that the things you place high value on are the things your kids will place high value on. If you tend to wing it, they will, too. Are there exceptions? Of course. But as a general rule,

the things you are telling your kids to do are being overpowered by the things they are watching you do!

One of the greatest ways to communicate values-based life

lessons to your kids is through stories. There are literally hundreds of studies showing how tying stories into a lesson significantly enhances the likelihood of the lesson taking hold in the life of the listener, regardless of age. When you are able to share a values-based life lesson through a story to your kids, it will be a lesson that sticks with them for decades and will support your legacy initiative.

Below are a couple of stories I shared with my sons while they were still living at home. I would personalize "The Worry Tree" to how my sons could or should deal with worry or trouble. For one thing, I wanted to convey that worry is normal. But secondly, I wanted them to understand that worry should never control them. My intent was to equip them with an outlet to deal with worry in a healthy way. Let's check it out:

"THE WORRY TREE"

The carpenter I hired to help me restore an old farmhouse had just finished a rough first day on the job. A flat tire made him lose an hour of work, his electric saw quit, and now his ancient pickup truck refused to start. While I drove him home, he sat in stony silence.

On arriving, he invited me in to meet his family. As we walked toward the front door, he paused briefly at a small tree, touching the tips of the branches with both hands. When opening the door, he underwent an amazing transformation. His tanned face wreathed in smiles and he hugged his two small children and gave his wife a kiss.

Afterward he walked me to the car. We passed the tree and my curiosity got the better of me. I asked him about what I had seen him do earlier.

"Oh, that's my trouble tree," he replied. "I know I can't help having troubles on the job, but one thing for sure, troubles don't belong in the house with my wife and the children. So, I just hang

them on the tree every night when I come home. Then in the morning, I pick them up again."

"Funny thing is," he smiled, "when I come out in the morning to pick 'em up, there ain't nearly as many as I remember hanging up the night before."

–Author unknown

"THE WORRY TREE" APPLICATION:

1. Much of our worry, stress, and anxiety is multiplied when we are tired and in a rest deficit. Having a proper amount of rest often allows for a positive shift in perspective;
2. Taking time to acknowledge the worries of life is a positive in our lives, not a negative;
3. You will never be able to address what is beyond your awareness. Said differently, you cannot address those things of which you aren't aware.

Another story I began sharing with my sons when they were in their upper teens and low twenties was "The Silver Sword & Gold Sword." This story demonstrates an instantaneous perspective shift from "boss mode" to "influencer mode." Granted, they didn't fully appreciate it until they were either in a leadership role professionally or they were married. The first place I discovered this nugget of knowledge, which I then turned into a story for my sons, was from the book, "The Hidden Value of a Man" by Gary Smalley and John Trent. It's a book primarily written for men in their role as husbands and fathers. But the lesson from this story transitions perfectly between your personal world and your business world, and is fitting for both men and women. I'll first provide a baseline description from the book and then share a little of how I morphed it into a story. The entire story is in Appendix C.

1) The Silver Sword has positional power, which is the clout, control, prestige, and authority that comes from where you work, what you do, your job title, and your resume; 2) The Gold Sword has personal power, which is the ability to develop meaningful, fulfilling relationships.

Leaving a positive legacy will always involve interacting with other people, predominantly with your own heirs. The Silver Sword is less diplomatic, more rigid, and usually more insistent that something gets done. The Gold Sword is more relational and ideally suited to perpetuate lasting, positive, trusting relationships. Being aware of the desired outcome allows for an intentional awareness of which sword to use at the moment to bring about the desired outcome.

CHAPTER APPLICATION

Reflection:

- As a parent, you are *always* on the clock; it's not "Did they see me?" but rather, "What did they see?"
- Values are more caught than taught.
- Repetition is one of the most effective ways to instill family values and behaviors.
- Lessons and values are best taught through stories.

Implementation:

- Complete the Core Values exercise for your personal top five values.
- Define the Core Values for the family.

5

LEG 3: KNOWLEDGE

"Knowledge is power. Information is power. The secreting or hoarding of knowledge or information may be an act of tyranny camouflaged as humility."

– Robin Morgan

So, if what Robin Morgan says is true, withholding knowledge from your heirs is akin to an act of tyranny? Wow, that's a pretty strong statement. The withholding of knowledge is one of the most overlooked items when intentionally passing things on to the next generation. One of the reasons information is missed is that you have likely developed and honed your particular skill set over many years and don't realize how unique and strong your skills are. Because it seems so natural to you now, it doesn't cross your mind that it's taken decades and likely many iterations to finally get to where you are, and you will need to start at square one if you're going to get your descendants up to speed.

Perhaps your skills are in the people and influence space. The same thing applies. What you are really good at wasn't just purely a natural thing; in other words, you weren't just born that way. It was something you probably had a natural bent towards but it still had to be honed over time. One of my sons wants me to create a course on networking. To be honest, it's proving to be a challenge to create because what I do that makes it easy seems like it should be common sense to everyone.

What proficiencies do you possess? If your wealth is tied to a business (or several), do you have a process in place to equip and empower your children, and your heirs, to effectively and efficiently take over the business(es) some day? This may be the most important leg of the legacy table to address. However, I tend to feel that way about whichever "leg" I'm working on at the moment. Seriously, many benefactors are literally addicted to the game of winning so much so that they fail to position their business, their potential legacy, to continue to win after they are gone.

This positioning I reference is in making sure those younger than you, and currently less capable than you are in your particular skill, are being trained to take over for you when you pass away. In fact, since we never know when our last day will be, the ideal scenario is having them *fully* capable of taking over well before they are called on to do so. Sometimes, control of the present is like a highly addictive drug. In such cases, being addicted to control in the now prevents us from adequately preparing others. This increases the likelihood that your heirs would not be ready to take over when the time comes. This leads to failure, and puts your family legacy at a very high risk of losing its influence just a generation or two from now.

Specialized knowledge is often nothing more than a lifetime of skills that have been adapted and improved upon over time. We often take our special knowledge for granted. It is usually something that we have done for so long, we no longer realize how special it is. It becomes second nature. How can you make sure that the next generation understands where this knowledge came from? How do you identify and put into words what the specialized knowledge even is?

Maybe think of it this way: if you were to create a job post for a new executive position within one of your businesses, what requirements would you expect? What type of experience would be required? Do you have a certain behavioral profile you would be looking for? Are there certain technical licenses or certifications required? This lack of specialized knowledge is a double-edged sword: it increases the perceived need for the older generation to maintain an iron-fisted control because the next generation just isn't ready; secondly, the longer control is clung to, the higher likelihood the family legacy will have only marginal impact and be very short-lived.

An alternate phrase for specialized knowledge is "intellectual capital." The best and simplest definition I have found is from "Investopedia": *Intellectual capital is the value of a company's employee knowledge, skills, business training, or any proprietary information that may provide the company with a competitive advantage.*

Now, think about your descendants who will take over the family business or businesses someday. Do they have a solid and legitimate grasp of what sets these companies apart in the industry? In other words, does your heir have the qualifications for the job post we discussed? If not, how can you get them ready? A little later, we'll explore ways to get heirs ready to transition and facilitate a true legacy company as opposed to just assuming a title when the time comes.

When I worked with high-net-worth families that primarily had their wealth in a family business, I often used the movie *Tommy Boy* as an example of what *not* to do and how *not* to prepare. Tommy was ill-equipped to take over the family company when his father suddenly passed away. Not only did that negatively impact the immediate family but it also put every family associated with the company at risk. Fortunately, consistency and intentionality will go a long way in solidifying the family business.

Yes, I know it was only a movie. But it is also real life. I have personal experiences of Tommy-like situations I could share. Unfortunately, the instances I'm aware of did not turn out as well as the TV version did.

So, I guess it begs the question: How does one go about transferring the necessary knowledge to the heirs to make sure the family business not only survives but continues to grow and increase the family's net worth?

Let's take a deeper look at some tactics the families that create, sustain, and increase multi-generational wealth by focusing on knowledge transfer to the next generation. Something we will see is that they were not primarily focused on restricting their heirs' access to the wealth using legal documents. Instead, for decades they were intentionally focusing on transferring their family's vision, values, and knowledge to future generations. Furthermore, their primary method of transferring these intangibles was by keeping their heirs within proximity of themselves and other key leaders in their organizations during important meetings and decision-making opportunities.

When the family elders, the creators and facilitators of the wealth, held important meetings, they made sure their heirs were in the audience. Their heirs were not necessarily part of the leadership team, unless they held a title, but they were somewhere in the room to listen and learn. They learned far more from being in the room, witnessing the dealings of the company, than anything else. Over time, they gradually learned how to handle both the concerns and the opportunities within the business. There is absolutely no way to learn these things in a classroom.

Ken Coleman, in his book, "The Proximity Principle", describes the proximity principle as a formula:

"The right people + The right places + The right practices = Great Opportunities"

While his book primarily focuses on intentionally choosing relationships to help you get to where you want to go or to land the job of your dreams, I'm applying the same formula to introduce a proven pattern of self-fulfillment and achievement to support an amazing family legacy. The family elders can use Coleman's proximity principle to be intentional at making sure their heirs, the right people, are in the right places and exposed to the right practices for long enough that it becomes ingrained into both their conscious and subconscious mind. In my opinion, the time to begin this practice is well before you think it is necessary.

In this example, proximity is about being "in the room" during as many meetings as possible. In those meetings, they are learning more than just tactical knowledge. They are also learning the nuances of leadership and decision making. They will be absorbing, through proximity, the early stages of learning to trust their gut. Oh, I get it, understanding reports like forecast models, balance sheets, and profit and loss statements are vitally important. These reports can highlight trends that should be addressed as well as opportunities to capitalize on. But some of the best decisions made in the life of a company won't be based purely on data.

It is not enough that your physical DNA is running throughout their body. There is also a legacy DNA, your specific knowledge, that is *not* automatically passed on to the next generation. This type of knowledge is typically not learned through formal education. Instead, it's what has been developed and acquired throughout the lifespan of the parents. The most effective and efficient method of transferring knowledge is intentional proximity. And *this*, my friends, is a great example of something more easily caught than taught.

But what if the knowledge you possess is more of a *foreknowledge* of things to come? Some might call this intuition or insight. Sometimes, though, you are given a glimpse into the future from someone else's perspective. Let me share an example of this unique gift of foreknowledge. In 1888, there were two brothers, Alfred and Ludvig, and one of them made life-altering decisions after his brother passed away. When Ludvig passed away, the journalist writing the obituary for his paper mistakenly wrote it as if it was Alfred who had died.

The journalist stated that the "Merchant of Death" had finally passed away. He went on to write that Alfred had gotten rich from his ability to "mutilate and kill" vast amounts of people at once. You see, Alfred was a war-time explosive munitions expert and became known as "The Dynamite King". This made him widely known, greatly feared, and very wealthy.

As Alfred read the obituary about himself, he apparently had an epiphany of how he would be remembered and he didn't like it. He decided to make immediate changes so that when he finally did pass, the words written about him would be vastly different. He supposedly rewrote his will to leave most of his vast wealth, $265 million in today's dollars, to a humanity-based cause or causes so that no one would be able to cast negative aspersions on his name at his death. His name was Alfred Nobel, and his legacy established the Nobel Peace Prize.

Chapter Application

Reflection:

- *"Knowledge is power. Information is power. The secreting or hoarding of knowledge or information may be an act of tyranny camouflaged as humility." - Robin Morgan*
- What skill or knowledge do you possess that feels so completely natural that you would have trouble explaining it to someone else?
- What skill or knowledge do you possess that gives you a competitive advantage in business or relationships?

Implementation:

- Write out, or dictate, what makes you so effective in what you do.
- Consider writing a job description to hire your replacement. What *must* they already know to fill your shoes immediately?
- Begin to implement the proximity principle before you think it is required.

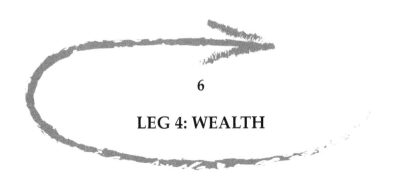

6

LEG 4: WEALTH

"All the breaks you need in life wait within your imagination, imagination is the workshop of your mind, capable of turning mind energy into accomplishment and wealth."

– Napoleon Hill

WEALTH TRANSFER IS OFTEN THE SIMPLEST to address because there is an entire industry built around this topic. It consists of financial planners and advisors, tax strategists, tax attorneys, trust & entity attorneys, and more.

RBC Wealth Management facilitated a detailed wealth and estate planning survey back in 2017. To qualify for their survey, participants had to have a minimum net worth of at least $4.5 million. To put this in proper perspective, the percentage of Americans considered a millionaire is only 8.8%, so $4.5 million isn't a small sum. What the survey found was, frankly, a little concerning. They found that only 54% of the respondents said they have a will. And while 26% said they have a full wealth transfer plan in place, a surprising 32% said they had done nothing to prepare yet. A more recent study by Caring.com shows the percentage of those not having even a basic will to be as high as 68%!

That same RBC Wealth Management study asked if these high-net-worth families had confidence their kids would be able to handle the family wealth once it was transferred at death. What they found was a direct correlation between the families that had full financial plans in place versus those who didn't. The greater the level of planning the elders did, the higher the level of confidence their kids could effectively handle the wealth. Those who hadn't done any planning showed the lowest level of confidence in their kids' ability to handle wealth.

But here is something else interesting from that study: as it turns out, Millennials are actually pretty darn good with their money. And, there is a great deal of polarization within the Millennial group. Some are outstanding at making money, creating amazingly successful businesses, and implementing strategies to hold on to it, while others are 180 degrees from that picture. But as far as percentages go, based on the study, a greater percentage of Millennials started taking money seriously at age twenty instead of age thirty-two like the Boomer generation. Further, a greater percentage of them also had full-blown financial plans in place as well, 38% versus 26%. So, even though many Boomers are currently keeping tight control on the assets for fear their heirs can't handle it, this study shows the opposite. The Millennial generation as a whole is quite capable of creating, handling, and protecting money.

In looking into the reason so many people choose not to implement such a basic planning tool, it was found that they felt it to be too emotionally challenging, time-consuming, discouraging, or not worth the financial expense required. In other words, they felt it was a greater inconvenience than the value of peace of mind brought by sorting out their personal and financial affairs. With that said, where do you stand? Which camp are you in? Would you rather be inconvenienced now or have your heirs deal with a much greater level of inconvenience later?

In the ideal scenario, you will either know of an attorney or have a trusted friend or advisor who can recommend an attorney to help you get the right documents in place. And I highly recommend doing it that way over what I'm writing next. But if you absolutely refuse to take the initiative and the time to meet with an attorney, at least take the time to search the internet for another option. There is honestly no excuse to choose to do nothing. You ARE better than that!

I know that may not have been received all that well by some. Maybe it was a bit too direct. But I said it because even without meeting you in person, I care about how well you do in leaving your legacy behind. I'll share with you what I shared with my sons: "I am not here to be popular! I'm here to help get you to the next level. And when you get to the next level, I'm pretty sure I'll be quite popular with you!" If possible, imagine me sitting right beside you, letting you know I'm preparing you for the next level. Let's make it happen. You got this."

Since I am no longer a licensed advisor, I will *not* be providing specific advice. Every family is different and warrants their own strategy with highly qualified advisors who are all working together to coordinate and implement your wishes. I will simply give some examples of a variety of high-net-worth families I worked with over the last several decades and the top four concerns that I would repeatedly come across.

Consistently, the first and most common concern was taxes. Nothing frustrated these high-net-worth families like the thought of the government being the biggest beneficiary of their decades of hard work. Speaking of a beneficiary, the beneficiary isn't required to be an actual physical, breathing person. It could involve other legal entities like trusts or corporations, in which you could allocate funds to different areas of focus and different timelines. Areas of focus could be charitable giving, philanthropic work, taking care of special needs heirs, balancing the inheritance between heirs involved in the business with those not in the business, and structuring and funding business buy/sell arrangements. There are a host of financial vehicles and legal documents that can come into play to facilitate just about anything you wish.

Over 40 years ago, Justice Learned Hand said, "In America, there are two tax systems; one for the informed and one for the uninformed. Both systems are legal." This may explain why some of the very wealthy pay a smaller percentage of their income towards taxes than those making only a fraction of the income than they are. If you are not currently incorporating trusts and/or corporations into your planning strategies as a high-net-worth individual or family, you may be missing out on some extremely beneficial planning strategies.

A consistent second concern arose with those families that had their assets mainly tied to a family business(es) where some of their heirs were involved in the business and some had no involvement whatsoever. In this scenario, we worked with what we called estate equalization plans. I personally witnessed families be all but torn apart due to a lack of planning in this particular lane. It would be unreasonable and unfair to leave the family business to all heirs equally, unless they were all active in the business already.

Through proper planning, there is a way to make sure all your heirs are treated as financial equals, even when you leave the business assets to your heirs in the business and assign the "newly-created assets" to those heirs not active in the business. These newly created assets are typically provided by either life insurance, annuities, or other investments. Every scenario is different, so if you have some of your heirs active in a family business and some that aren't, there are usually ways to equalize the wealth to be transferred.

The third most consistent issue to arise was where family

assets were predominantly in raw land, especially things like timber and agriculture in the South. In the event that the vast majority of the wealth was in land, this scenario could create a massive estate tax bill and yet have little to no cash to pay the government. In cases like this, the government didn't have any problem forcing liquidation upon the family, even if it required rock-bottom pricing referred to as a "fire sale." This equated to a forced sale of the very assets that were driving the tax bill in the first place. I remember one situation where the family ended up having to discount their land asset down to $7 million from nearly $9 million just to get the quick sale. In essence, because of the need to sell quickly, they had to sell $9 million worth of land to cover the $7 million tax bill. I will cover this example in more detail in Chapter 13.

The fourth most common topic was their philanthropic desires. These ideas ranged from wanting to support their local church, to creating an endowment at their alma mater, to setting up ongoing funding for causes of a particular nonprofit. These causes involved things like cancer and Alzheimer's research, inner-city support, and the humane society, just to name a few. In all instances, there were unique strategies available to those who started the planning process early and were also in good health.

For those in good health, your advisors have some financial products that may be able to drastically increase the amount of the financial gift at death. I remember one such family that was able to "donate" almost all their wealth to a qualified charity to minimize taxes, but because of their advanced planning and great health, their heirs were still able to receive virtually their entire inheritance as they replaced the amount donated with a corresponding amount of life insurance. If you are philanthropically minded, please do yourself a favor and get a referral to a professional who truly understands your desires and see what options are available.

These may be the four issues I came across the most, but there are countless other topics or categories to cover. What concerns you the most when it comes to your wealth? More specifically, what concerns you the most about the wealth transfer process? Besides you, who knows the full extent of your wealth and your preference for how it will one day be transferred and to whom? The worst time for families to be asking these questions is after the death of a loved one. There is enough stress going on in those moments without also being concerned with how many assets are involved, where they are, and whether plans and processes are in place to smoothly, efficiently, and effectively transfer control and authority to the heirs to negate a break in the process.

There are a plethora of trusts and other legal documents that allow you to transfer your wealth in any form or fashion you desire, and in as many different percentages as you have individuals or organizations you want to leave something to...and yes, even pets! The key is to partner with the proper wealth transfer professionals. By proper, I am not referring to those with just the proper licenses and credentials. I would personally recommend getting personal referrals from folks you already know and trust. Even then, I would encourage you to interview more than one and look for a solid, personal fit.

What about families where there wasn't enough wealth to be concerned about estate taxes? Do they still need to do some basic planning? Absolutely, YES! More times than I can count, I was made aware of some great, middle-income families where one or two of the heirs were far more aggressive than the other heirs when it came to what they felt was rightfully theirs. In those situations, they obviously felt justified in taking a significantly larger portion of what little there was. And maybe they were justified, but then again, maybe they weren't. So yes, regardless of the size of the estate, the best thing you can do is ensure your wishes are clearly documented with an objective third party.

Because once you're gone, absent proper documentation, your influence and input is clearly over.

But the scope of this book is more about covering those first three areas I mentioned: Vision, Values, and Knowledge, in greater detail. Besides, those three areas are vastly overlooked and often taken for granted. They are also the most likely to determine *if* the wealth transition and protection strategies implemented will help the assets last to the second and third generations and beyond. Solid wealth transfer vehicles and legal documents are not enough to overcome a lack of intentionally transferring the family vision, values, and the specialized knowledge acquired in creating the wealth in the first place.

CHAPTER APPLICATION

Reflection:

- The most basic planning tool is creating the Last Will and Testament. But studies show a large percentage of the population does not have that document in place, even within the high-net-worth families.
- Top concerns triggering the necessary planning: 1) Taxes; 2) Family business(es); 3) Majority of assets are in raw land; 4) Philanthropic desires.
- Where are you in the process? There is no excuse for choosing to do nothing.

Implementation:

- If you don't have a will, set a target date of 90 days from now to rectify that. If you do have a will, have there been any family or business changes that would warrant having it updated?

7

THE FULL LEGACY PICTURE

"The greatest legacy one can pass on to one's children and grandchildren is not money or other material things accumulated in one's life, but rather a legacy of character and faith."

– Billy Graham

STUDIES HAVE SHOWN HOW we live and the choices we make can impact at least the next five generations. What could possibly be the long-term impact of a family that was highly intentional with modeling and communicating their values to their children and to their children's children versus a family with absolutely no intentionality? Great question! Fortunately, there are a couple of very well-documented studies on this very topic: one by educational journalist, A.E. Winship and one by a scholar, Benjamin B. Warfield from Princeton.

THE INTENTIONAL FAMILY, JONATHAN AND SARAH EDWARDS.

Jonathan and Sarah were married in 1727 and went on to

have 11 children. Firsthand accounts found that each night, Jonathan would spend at least one hour conversing with his family and then he would pray an individual blessing over each child at bedtime.

The timeline of the study took a look at the five generations 150 years after Jonathan's death in 1758. What they found was quite amazing. Within those 150 years, they found the following in the Edwards lineage:

- 1 U.S. Vice President
- 1 Dean of a law school
- 1 Dean of a medical school
- 3 U.S. Senators
- 3 Governors
- 3 Mayors
- 13 College Presidents
- 30 Judges
- 60 Doctors
- 65 Professors
- 75 Military Officers
- 80 Public Office Holders
- 100 Lawyers
- 100 Clergymen
- 285 College Graduates

The total number of Edwards descendants was nearly 1,400 individuals. This impressive lineage was a result of a husband and wife who were highly intentional to model *and* communicate their values to their children and grandchildren on a regular basis.

THE NON-INTENTIONAL FAMILY, MAX JUKES.

In contrast with the Edwards family, let's look at another

well-known, five generation study for the lineage of Max Jukes. This study involved researching the over 1,200 descendants of Max Jukes. Within this 150 year span, you'll find the following:

- 7 convicted murders
- 60 thieves
- 190 prostitutes
- 150 other convicts
- 310 paupers at death
- 440 who were wrecked by addiction to alcohol
- 300 who died prematurely

*Very little can be found out about Max Jukes' wife, other than "he married a woman similar to himself." He was described as an atheist and a man with little distinction between what was good or evil.

According to the study on Max Jukes, there was not one single descendant found to have had a positive contribution to the state of New York. Not even one! Within the last decade, the state of New York did a financial impact study of the Jukes family from this same time frame. They found that instead of contributing to society, the Jukes family actually cost the state over $1,200,000 (not adjusted to current day value).

These two studies are not alone in their findings, but they are the most well known. These two studies also created the framework for what has become known as the Five-Generation Rule.

The Five Generation Rule can be summed up as the following:

"How a parent raises their child — the love they give, the values they teach, the emotional environment they offer, the education they provide — influences not only their children but the four generations to follow, either for good or evil."

Doing Something for Yourself versus for Others

Studies show that becoming aware of your current legacy is the first step in impacting your future legacy. The older you become, the more you realize that every day is a gift. This is not to come across as morbid. Quite the contrary. When we realize that each day is a gift, we are more likely to live our days intentionally and enjoy them. And if we happen to give our legacy any thought at all, we will realize that we are in complete control of how that turns out as well. Your legacy *is* within your control.

Why is control important? Studies have shown "power" (control) plays a slightly different role in the realm of leaving a legacy than in everyday life. Actually, the timeframe is the real differentiator. Lord Acton, a British politician in the 19th century, said, "absolute power corrupts absolutely." Lord Acton surmised that the timeline between power and corruption is "nearly immediate, present-tense, or at least the effects are felt relatively quickly."

When power is viewed from the perspective of intergenerational beneficence, the focus is on leaving a better future for the heirs than the one delivered for you. When we realize that our legacy *is* fully, 100%, within our power to create, studies show you will make decisions that will benefit future generations rather than focusing on yourself in the present. Further, while you are focusing on leaving your heirs an inheritance, your life in the here and now *and* your legacy (reputation) will both be improved.

Burden vs Benefit

When it comes to intentionally and positively impacting your legacy, what is your motive? And by motive, I'm not implying one is right and one is wrong. Rather, when the focus is to prevent a future *burden* instead of creating a future *benefit*, one's power is more likely to be used for the benefit of others *over* benefiting self. It has been statistically shown that preventing a future burden has a much greater influence on decisions that affect the future. So, when you focus on creating your own legacy, think about relieving, lifting, or negating a future burden to help you stay the course and implement your plans.

SETTING THE STAGE

Do you recall from earlier the turning point for Alfred Nobel? His obituary. He had the unfortunate opportunity of reading his own obituary, which was written about him, in error, instead of his recently deceased brother. It turned out to be a wake-up call and it prompted him to set a new course for how he was to be remembered. Naturally, his late course correction didn't negate his destructive contributions to the world up to that point, but it did set the stage to create a new story. It allowed for future generations to think more fondly of the creator of the Nobel Peace prize.

I've heard there are actually three potential legacy outcomes when I pass:

1. I am not remembered at all. I did nothing. I stood for nothing, I simply existed. Yes, there may be a few people at the funeral but even they won't give any thought about me after just one or two weeks;

2. I am remembered in a very negative light. It could be something as simple as being remembered as a grumpy, stingy, irritable old man with no friends. Or it could be something significantly worse...the type of things movies are made of;

3. I am sorely missed for decades or even centuries to come. In

this scenario, I was intentional to leave my mark on humanity. Not so much that I wanted to be remembered well, but because I genuinely wanted to add value and make an impact all the way to the very end.

Of these three scenarios, only number three is the mark of someone with a generational consciousness. But I feel I could probably add a fourth outcome. On the surface, it resembles number three with its intentionality. But in reality, scenario number three is actually all about being remembered well and secondarily about them adding value to others. They believe in Malcolm Forbes' famous line, "He who dies with the most toys wins." This perspective is more of a narcissistic viewpoint for wanting your legacy to outlive you. But *I* say, "He who dies with the most toys still dies."

Here is a possible fourth type of legacy outcome:

4. I consistently put the betterment of others ahead of myself. I was incredibly intentional to make sure my own family members understood, honored, and respected my values and vision for our family name. My family name is synonymous with integrity, faith, wealth, and philanthropy. My entire genealogy, from oldest to youngest, is treated with respect and prepared for greatness, but without the pressure to perform to be loved and respected as a part of our family. Regardless of their involvement in the family businesses, they will be loved and always have a seat at my table. Processes are in place to prepare my family name to remain excellent and extend into perpetuity.

Look to Your Future to Create Your Present

"A good character is the best tombstone. Those who loved you and were helped by you will remember you when forget-me-nots have withered. Carve your name on hearts, not on marble."

- Charles Spurgeon

Have you ever sat down and written out your own eulogy or obituary? Some think it might be a bit too morbid to do. I, however, see it as a tool to help clarify how you want to be remembered, if remembered at all. This exercise literally allows you to go out into the future twenty, forty, or seventy years and dream about all that you will be able to accomplish during that time. If you think through this exercise deeply and in detail, it can impact you at an emotional level and change the trajectory of your life. Recall how the Nobel prize came about? While Alfred Nobel didn't intentionally sit down to write his own eulogy, he was privileged to have someone do it on his behalf and it changed everything for him.

I encourage you to give this exercise a go. First, either get out a sheet of paper and grab a pen, or open your computer or tablet, and prepare to get honest with yourself on how you would like your life to be remembered–or the organizations you want to build or the people with whom you really want to have a lasting impact. At this stage, it's only for you. No one else will see it. So, get ready to dream big. Carve out some quiet time to get really clear on what you want to be said when you're gone. It is this level of clarity that will allow you to begin the intentional road to legacy building.

To get started, think about what you would *like* to be said at your funeral. For today, let's not worry whether those statements are true at this time or not. To do this exercise right, you must start with the end in mind. It allows you to reverse engineer how to make it happen after you are clear on what "the end" could and should look like.

I'm sure you've been to a funeral before, but still, I'll share a few questions below to help get your thoughts going:

- What is your full name? (see, we're starting off really, really easy)
- How many years did you live?
- What do you want to be known for (personally, professionally, philanthropically)?
- What will your loved ones say on your behalf?
- What do your closest friends recall as some of your finest qualities?

Answering the above questions will take you anywhere from five to 30 minutes. Remember: what you come up with during this exercise will be the foundation you can begin "living into" immediately. Listen, if you take this exercise seriously, you will likely feel a real emotion welling up inside of you as you are writing down your answers. Secondly, when you have clarity *and* emotion, something happens to you at a subconscious level. Without cognitively focusing on your daily decisions, your subconscious person will begin to make decisions that actually align with actions and behaviors consistent with becoming that person you just wrote about.

From here, you simply take the answers to the above questions and begin to put them in paragraph form. To help create the picture for you, I created a hypothetical sample of answering the questions *and* then will put it into paragraph form to give you a more visual track to run on.

Here you go:

- **What is your full name?** *Jane Nicole Doe*
- **How many years did you live?** *93*

- **What do you want to be known for (personally, professionally, philanthropically)?** *Jane was the youngest of X children. Jane was married for 72 years when her husband, Jacob, passed away two years ago. Jane is survived by xxxxx. Jane had a real passion for singing, the opera, and bringing joy to others, especially children.*
- **What will your loved ones say on your behalf?** *Jane was loving, kind, giving, generous, gifted.*
- **What do your closest friends recall as some of your finest qualities?** *I knew Jane for nearly 50 years. And during that time, I knew her to be....*

I will skip the obligatory statement of who predeceased whom, who was left behind and just get to the creative life-encouraging portion.

Jane accomplished so very much in her 93 years on this earth. Spending 72 of those years in marriage is only part of her amazing story. Jane was the most gentle soul, and the kindest woman who ever lived. Jane made friends and helped people every opportunity she had. She led a truly heroic, unique, and joy-filled life.

Jane studied music, singing, and opera at the "XYZ Conservatory" in Anytown, USA. She became one of the few singers alive to master the old knowledge of the "Bologna School" singing technique which allowed her to be heard with her natural voice over the orchestra without a microphone.

For over forty years, she also performed as a clown for many charity events, including her local Ronald McDonald House for terminally ill children. She felt bringing joy and laughter to children was one of creation's greatest healing resources. The children and parents loved her dedication beyond words. Jane was a firm believer of giving of one's time, talent, and resources for the good of others.

In her later years, Jane turned to writing, with a passionate desire to share her heart and accumulated experiences for the good of others. Her life is truly inspiring. Jane's passion for life and intentional desire to leave a lasting legacy is an inspiration to us all and will be deeply missed.

An online periodical, *The Business Journal*, ran an article in 2014 entitled, "Do this exercise to consider the life you should be leading". A much shorter title might have been, "Write your own eulogy to shape your life". Any way, they broke it down into three simple steps:

Step 1: Write the eulogy of the life you have already lived.
Step 2: Write the eulogy of the life you would have loved to have lived, the one that asserts your goals and dreams have come true.
Step 3: Compare the two and write about which inspires you more.

This is a simple, yet awakening exercise. You will never be able to address that of which you are not aware. When focusing on your legacy, you will not be able to impact the trajectory of your life until you take inventory of where you are right now. This is one of those exercises that is a total win-win. If by chance, your current life story is perfect, and cannot get any better, or the eulogy of the life you've already lived is exactly the way you want it to be, this exercise will be a confirmation that you're doing everything right. However, if your current eulogy of your life-to-date falls a little short of your ideal message, *now* you can identify it and begin making little changes here and there.

When you become clear on what you really want for your legacy and why, your choices and behavior begin to almost automatically fall in line with the actions and decisions required to attain the desired outcome.

Once you get clear on what you want, a change takes place within you. The clarity you now have on the inside begins to show up on the outside. In other words, because of your enhanced clarity of your desired future (internal), you just naturally choose to do things differently today (external) that will get you closer to or at the desired outcome in the future. You can use this eulogy exercise to gain a clearer picture of where you are today, as well as a reference point for whether anything should change to create the legacy you desire.

CHAPTER APPLICATION

Reflection:

- Two family names were contrasted from a legacy perspective; Jonathan Edwards and Max Jukes. How these two men lived and influenced their families mattered for generations.
- When focused on creating a positive legacy for others, you create a greater impact than focusing purely on yourself.

Implementation:

- Consider what you would like said at your own funeral and write it out.
- Is there a burden or challenge within your control that if NOT addressed during your lifetime will force your heirs to deal with it in theirs? How/When can you deal with it so they will not have to?

8

RELATIONSHIPS RULE

"As a child, the family that I had and the love I had from my two parents allowed me to go ahead and be more aggressive, to search and to take risks knowing that, if I failed, I could always come home to a family of love and support."

– Tiger Woods

I LOVE THE MESSAGE BEHIND this quote. Is Tiger Woods perfect as an adult? No, but no one is. However, the lesson I glean from that one sentence was that he knew he was loved, was encouraged to pursue his best, and *when* he failed, he knew his family would always be his biggest supporters. When a child is chastised, ridiculed, or embarrassed for failing or falling short, we actually teach the wrong lesson. The wrong lesson is that playing safe and not growing is better than shooting for higher targets and falling short.

The stark contrast in familial relationships within the Edwards family as opposed to the Jukes, when we consider the effect it had on society for generations, speaks to the importance of such relationships. With the Edwards family, Jonathan

Edwards was not only highly deliberate, but also willing to be inconvenienced by his intentional nightly routine. No doubt, there were plenty of other things to do with his evenings than spending his personal time every single night with each child. The Jukes family on the other hand, was pretty much a family in sharing the same last name and that was about it. There seemed to be no intentional effort made to increase unity within the family.

And then, we have an organization go to the effort to compile the respective ancestral lines of both the Edwards and Jukes family over a 150-year span to see the impact their families had on society. What we find is a massive difference. It appears Edwards' inconveniences paid off for his family line as well as for society. No doubt, his children were a byproduct of his and Sarah's intentionality.

It was Carl Jung who said, "Children are educated by what the grown-up is and not by his talk." Technically, I agree with his assertion. But it almost implies that the words we speak as parents aren't all that important. I'm sure if I had the opportunity to sit down and interview Carl Jung, he would clearly state that while actions may speak louder than words, the real power of influence as a parent is when our words and our actions are in alignment.

There are no guarantees in life. But one thing I believe is as close to a guarantee as one can get is that there is tremendous value in investing in family relationships–especially when those relationships are your sons and daughters first, as well as other extended family. Strong family relationships facilitate a deeper level of trust amongst all parties. When you go about being intentional in building strong family relationships for decades, it will make the transition of leadership from one generation to the next significantly smoother. The senior generation will feel more in control by handing over the reins to their heirs and transitioning out and not feeling like they are being forced out.

If you remember earlier in the book, we discussed the challenge of the younger generation taking over the family business without being adequately prepared. This happens when they haven't had decades to rise through the ranks, sit in on countless leadership meetings, and build highly intentional trusting relationships. The strength of these relationships allows for all parties to view the transition as something being done *for* me and not *to* me. Absent strong relationships, it is far more likely that all parties feel they aren't being heard, are getting the short end of the stick, and even being disrespected through the transition process.

These types of relationships take time. I have a variety of ideas to build and strengthen familial relationships. Some of the ideas I will share are things we implemented when our boys were younger. Some are ideas I've shared with my sons now that they are adults, regarding certain things that I'd do differently today. Either way, strong family relationships are rarely, if ever, created by accident. They take effort. They take intentionality. They take a willingness to be inconvenienced now for a bigger, stronger, and brighter future.

RELATIONSHIP BUILDING IDEAS:

The tragedy of what took place on what is now simply referred to as 9/11, birthed one of our family's first, intentional family-relationship-building activities. I have yet to use the phrase "9/11" in a personal setting where I don't see something shift in the other person's body language or a simple change in their eyes. If you are old enough, there's a very strong likelihood that you can remember exactly where you were when it happened as well. The reason? Emotion enhances recall because it creates a bond between you and the event that makes it memorable.

My wife was concerned with how our three boys were going

to process what had happened. They were around the ages of twelve, nine, and seven. Knowing our boys loved fires and they loved to eat, especially things made on said fire, I bought a wood-burning chiminea, which is an older version of today's common fire pit. The chiminea was a tall clay structure with a single opening about twelve to fifteen inches across. It was large enough to put decent sized pieces of wood in it. This required that we all sit side-by-side in a semi-circle, facing the fire. What we learned was that if we provided both food and fire, they would sit and communicate with us for one to two hours.

This became our ritual almost every Sunday evening until it got too hot outside. We affectionately called these nights our "Fireside Chats". We honestly had no idea that what we would implement as a result of 9/11 would last for years, and still be thought about fondly into their adulthood, and be the spring-board into being highly intentional in growing our family rela-tionships. During those early days, we would at times allow them to grill their dinner over the fire as we discussed various topics like school, sports, girls, church, God, 9/11, and anything else that could possibly pop up in a young boy's mind. I realize now that these were the early days of intentionally training our sons to think critically and communicate for themselves.

"The greatest gifts you can give your children are the roots of responsibility and the wings of independence."

– Denis Waitley

After reading the book, "Raising a Modern Day Knight" by Robert Lewis, I recognized the importance of the intentional rite of passage for my sons. There were several transition periods and activities we implemented as a result of what I learned. One activity was once they turned 13, I would check them out of school and take them to either leadership events like the John

Maxwell Maximum Impact Simulcast or have them tag along with me when I was doing a speaking engagement so they could "help me carry things." My intention was that they became somewhat comfortable being around leaders and other successful people. I wanted them to have a healthy respect for the success of others and not be intimidated by it.

Another thing we implemented within a year or two is something I cover in greater detail in Chapter 11 called The Annual Family Vision Cast. For now, I'll just share a little about how some of the first ones went to give you an idea of how simple getting started can be. What I share with you in Chapter 11 is an actual template of what we ended up with after years of trial and error. For our first Family Vision Cast, we went to a local coffee house on a Saturday afternoon and talked through a simple one-page document with some very simple, basic questions. We honestly had no idea of what to expect, but we sure had fun doing it together!

For years, I traveled extensively with my job. It wasn't uncommon for me to leave early Monday morning and return home Thursday evening. I would do this type of travel six to seven weeks out of every eight. There were times that I would get concerned that if something happened to me with all that travel, that my boys may not know what all I stood for and how important they were to me. At the end of each year, I would write each of them a personal letter that I had set aside in a special folder. These were the type of letters that I hoped they would never see because they were one of those "in case I'm gone" letters.

Obviously, I'm still here, praise God! But this leads me to share what I've recommended to my oldest son to do differently for his kids. At the end of each year, I would write a new letter and toss the one from the previous year. I didn't think about what amazing value it would be to have all those letters available to read at their eighteenth birthday or prior to getting married.

So what I've recommended to my son who already has kids, is to allow them to pile up year after year. It may also be more advisable today to do a video letter and store the video in a safe or something.

As of this writing, my sons are all out on their own, starting their own families and doing quite well. What I'm most proud of is the relationship we all have with one another, and it's taken a lot of work from all parties. Something I do for them once or twice a year is just write them a letter or email sharing how important they are to me. How important my wife and faith are to me. I intentionally speak life and encouragement into them. What I've learned is it doesn't matter how old my sons get, they will always value and appreciate their dad pursuing a relationship with them. Outside of my faith in God, nothing is more important to me than my family relationships.

And now that I have grandkids, pretty soon I'll be starting the practice of writing letters to them as well. I *will* be remembered as a highly intentional patriarch. My legacy will be one of faith and family as a top priority. I will *not* leave this earth having left a strong relationship with my family merely to chance. And because you've made it this far in the book, you must feel the same way.

Now, I don't know what stage of life you are in currently. But obviously, the topic of legacy is important to you. H. Jackson Brown, Jr. said, "Live so that when your children think of fairness, caring, and integrity, they think of you." Being aware of the current caliber of your family relationships *and* having a pretty clear picture of the quality you desire of your family relationships will allow you to begin intentionally implementing ideas and activities to reach the desired outcome. It doesn't matter how old you or your heirs are at the moment. You are never too young nor too old to begin improving those relationships that are most important to you.

One thing I consistently noticed was there was a direct correlation between the strength of the family relationships and the smooth transition of assets. The stronger the relationships, the smoother the transition of the estate. Even in those instances where things were not simple, clear cut, nor all assets were divided equally–where strength of relationship had been a priority, calmer heads prevailed.

CHAPTER APPLICATION

Reflection:

- A child who knows they are loved and not looked down on when they fail will feel more comfortable striving to be all they can become instead of playing it safe to prevent failing.
- Writing personal letters to family members is a timeless way to convey important messages, regardless of how old your kids are.
- Strong, healthy relationships allow for a smoother, more efficient transfer of control and ownership when there is a transition of assets.

Implementation:

- With kids still at home, even teenagers, be intentional to pick activities that are able to capture their attention for longer than 10-15 minutes; make sure the activities are for their interests and not your own.
- Consider writing a personal letter to those who are vitally important to you, regardless of age.
- With children still in the home, begin writing year-end letters and set them all aside to "gift" at some date in the future.

9

FOCUS ON YOUR HOUSEHOLD

"I think history is inextricably linked to identity. If you don't know your history, if you don't know your family, who are you?"

– Mary Pipher

BEFORE GOING ON ANY FURTHER about intentionally creating a legacy that outlives the five-generation pattern mentioned earlier, we should focus on those considered our immediate family first.

In this chapter we will only focus on intra-family relationships and then end with a simple exercise to identify the various areas we'd like to invest into the immediate next generation of relationships within your household. Notice that investing in the next generation is *not* limited to your own kids. Many I work with are taking the liberty to invest in others outside of their immediate family, but still of the same general age group. You'll notice I only reference my own biological kids, but understand these activities could easily encompass more than just my own kids.

In fact, one of the greatest exercises I did with my sons was enlisting other dads to help share wisdom. It's amazing how someone else could say virtually the same thing as me, sometimes even the exact same thing, and my sons would suddenly find the wherewithal to listen and be excited to share with me what they had learned from my friend. But the greater lesson was that the men I selected to speak into them had a totally different upbringing, with different stories and different experiences than I did. If I insisted on being the only source of life experiences for my sons to learn from, they would have missed out on skills and insights I would have had no way of depositing into them. So if you find your own children, even grown children, aren't really interested in listening to and learning from you, you may want to bring in others of similar age to invest into them. Oftentimes this can be a catalyst in getting your own kids' attention.

How would you describe your relationship with your kids? No matter how you choose to rate the relationship as it is today, it can likely become better. Do you *want* a better relationship with them? Are you willing to release some of the control within the relationship with the expectation that it can improve?

For this exercise, get your pen and paper ready and write down the following: **Things I want my kids to know or be equipped to do.** If you're married, this is a great exercise for couples. If you are not married, do *not* let that fact hinder you from taking this exercise just as seriously as those who are married. In fact, as a single parent, this is likely even more important!

For example, some of the things I wanted my sons to know or know how to do were how to think for themselves, understand how to set goals, how to be comfortable around leaders and people of influence, how to change a tire, and how to study their Bible, just to name a few. To jumpstart you in creating your own list, please check out Appendix B for a more extensive list.

There is no "right" number of items that should be on your

list. My initial list was probably only 12-15 bullet points but it grew over time to be over 50. From a psychological perspective, taking the time to complete this exercise drastically increases the likelihood of those items being taught to or caught by your heirs, even unintentionally. As you make your list, both at a conscious and subconscious level, your mind recognizes what is important to you and will begin to align your behavior to reinforce what's important. And since all lessons are indeed more caught than taught, you will begin to subconsciously model your actions for others to see and to imitate.

Another thing to consider for your list is age appropriateness. Those with younger children will have a list that looks a good bit different than someone with older teens. The beautiful thing about creating your own list as your kids are relatively young is that you will continually update your list as they grow. An ideal time to update your list is prior to your annual Family Vision Cast or your Family Legacy Retreat. I'll cover both of these annual activities soon.

LEGACY TREASURE AND LEGACY BAGGAGE

In the book, "The Intentional Legacy", David McAlvany used five words that really caught my attention: Legacy Treasure and Legacy Baggage. It spun off my own thinking of how I view and interpret my own ancestry.

For example, let's assume you were born into a dysfunctional family that had no legacy goals and you have never once received any type of financial inheritance. Meanwhile, some of your friends have received significant inheritances. You will learn nothing from your hardship if you play the victim card. If "woe is me" or "life just isn't fair" is your typical response, you will virtually guarantee that your heirs will not receive a worthwhile legacy from you either. However, if you choose differently–to be intentional and proactive about your legacy, vowing to create a positive legacy, *you* can break the cycle of perpetuating a negative legacy.

While reverse engineering is looking way out into the future and then working backward, sometimes it's equally beneficial to look way back into the past to address any lingering baggage. Legacy baggage is anything unhealed, unredeemed, negative, or burdensome that could trigger an unhealthy response in you or your family members. Just remember, you are not defined by your past, especially if you are able to learn from it. If this statement is true, it's even more true that you are not to be defined by the past of previous generations. Learning from your past, whether they are your mistakes or the mistakes of others, is a choice you must make to set a new trajectory for yourself and your heirs.

Some of the most successful families I have ever met are those that dealt well with a lot of generational baggage. But in turn, some of the most unsuccessful families I have ever met also had a lot of baggage, but they failed to deal well with it. Every family has baggage. It's how you view it that matters. You may view your generational lineage as not doing you any favors. That's the wrong perspective.

This conversation reminds me of many of the leadership lessons and discussions I had with my boys while they were growing up. I used to tell them that every leader they had was good for them. While some "leaders" were literally horrible, others were amazing. With the right perspective, they could learn from them both. There were some leaders my sons could vow to never be like. And they had other leaders whom they should do all they could to emulate. That perspective was designed to prevent them from ever being a victim. Yes, sometimes they were treated unfairly. Yes, sometimes they were taken advantage of. But at the end of the day, it was up to them to determine how they viewed and processed the negative experience.

If you're looking for them, there will always be a litany of life lessons from which to learn. There will be some of you reading this that have a legacy treasure trove of wonderful lessons on which to lean and from which to launch. There are others who have been going through the process of off-loading legacy baggage for years. For those of you off-loading baggage, please stay the course! It's so very worth it!

Let me explain it this way: as long as you run from the baggage, or hide from your baggage, or even blame others for your baggage, you will find your energy is almost supernaturally drawn to the negative baggage. Once you own it, however, you are remarkably set free from it. Only then will you be resourced to offload all of that old baggage. If we are not careful, when we fail to own the negative baggage that was handed down to us from a previous generation, we will inevitably be handing down the same things to our heirs, or at least something very similar. If we aren't able to own it and continue to remain the victim, we will be held hostage by a generation that is no longer around. We are called to be better than that.

I am *not* saying that you should accept the blame for previous generations. And I most definitely do not want you to adopt a "woe is me, it's all my fault" mindset. In reality, accepting blame for something that was actually handed down to you from a previous generation is martyrdom. Martyrdom is its own reward. Choosing to be a martyr is intentionally playing the victim card. However, taking ownership of the baggage is putting you in a position of control. Once you are in control, changes can be made. Understand, when I reference making changes, that is representative of changing a direction and then sticking with the change over an extended period of time. Making a change today rarely will create a different result tomorrow–unless it's something supernatural.

Recognize that creating a favorable legacy is done over the long haul. Just like starting a workout plan today doesn't give me the body I want tomorrow. Taking the necessary steps today toward the legacy I want will take years to fully implement. Be patient with yourself, and with your immediate family. It will take time. But the good news is that no matter where you are today, taking ownership is the most empowering choice you can make to set, or reset, the correct trajectory of your future legacy.

PERSONAL AUDIT

Another opportunity in working backward is to conduct a personal audit of the inheritance you have received. By inheritance, I'm referring to both the tangible and the intangible. Arguably, the gifts of greatest importance are the intangible. Examples of the tangible include both real assets as well as personal property. Personal property is made of real estate, raw land, and the physical property of businesses, to name a few. But the intangibles are things like: culture, values, vision, living memories, family history, and anything else that is very difficult on which to place a dollar valuation.

Many will look at their legacy, either what they have received or what they plan to pass on, as purely tangible. By this point, I trust that you are in agreement with me that it's the intangible that has the greatest impact on creating the tangible and making it last from generation to generation.

During this personal audit, take account of what has been passed along. If your audit turns up a lot of positive things, realize the effort that went into making that happen. Then using that data, how can you either grow it *or* further imbed that into your own legacy plans? If, on the other hand, what you found was *not* positive, what will you do differently to alter the course of events within your lifetime? You will rarely be able to address those things of which you aren't aware.

With the personal audit, you are looking backward to help determine how you would like to proceed. As we've already discussed, much of what I'm asking you to do will be inconvenient. Winston Churchill once said, "The farther backward you look, the farther forward you are likely to see." Often, in looking backward, you will have a new appreciation for the level of intentionality it will take to chart a new and much better course for yourself and your family.

When working on your personal audit, people sometimes find themselves disappointed by the baggage that's uncovered. Identifying baggage has a tendency to create and feed a victim mentality, as I mentioned earlier. To be clear, there are plenty of things in each of our lives that aren't fair. And as long as we allow it, those things can continue to hold us back. The most efficient way to break free from the baggage of your past is to simply own it. Yes, own the baggage you inherited. You cannot effectively deal with something that is not yours. I know this was discussed earlier, but it bears repeating.

CHAPTER APPLICATION

Reflection:

- You can learn and grow from both your legacy treasure and your legacy baggage.
- In the event of negative baggage, the moment you own it, you are set free from it and able to move forward.

Implementation:

- Regardless of the age of your heirs, become clear about what traits, characteristics, and skills you would like for them to possess (see Appendix B).

10

WHEN THINGS HAVEN'T GONE AS HOPED

"The pessimist complains about the wind; the optimist expects it to change; the realist adjusts the sails."

– Willam Arthur Ward

A HUGE PART OF LIFE and business is dealing with, and overcoming challenges, setbacks, and outright failures. How you frame these inevitable setbacks, large or small, will determine how well and how quickly you come out of that negative situation. Studies show a very clear delineation between having a positive bent versus having a neutral to negative bent. Multiple studies, including The Heart and Soul Study by Moskowitz, et al., and Optimism and Cardiovascular Health by Boehm, et al., both published in 2015, show a positive outlook is even linked to living longer. It is also linked with lower accounts of dementia. So a healthier, more positive perspective on life, especially during life's setbacks, positions you to overcome those challenges as well as live a longer, healthier life.

Failure is considered by the most successful among us as a precursor to success when viewed as a step toward growth and learning. This perspective is widely accepted in business. But it can also apply in the identification and creation of your ideal legacy. You may have children or grandchildren with incredible potential but they aren't doing anything intentional to live up to it. Many wealthy families I have worked with either accommodated poor behavior or brushed them aside and did life without them. Remember, being a strong patriarch or matriarch is incredibly inconvenient. But accommodating or enabling poor behavior will prove even more inconvenient years from now when you would like to have a strong heir taking over the reins for the family name.

How you frame or visualize failure is vitally important. When you view failure or setbacks as things done *to* you, you are viewing yourself as a victim. "Things done *to* you" frames it as something having complete control over you. If you perceive you have no control over a situation, you probably believe you have little to no control over how to get out of said situation. As we discussed earlier, proximity to a solid, steadfast group of individuals who won't allow you to play the victim card is priceless. Granted, we will most likely all have moments of discouragement or despair. Just make sure you don't set up residence there.

The alternative view is to view every failure or setback as something done *for* you. When you purposely view something as done *for* you, no matter how horrific, you will eventually muster the energy to fight your way *out* of the feeling of failure. I've met people that, after hearing their story, I feel they have every right to see something as being done *to* them. Some have endured unbelievably harsh and mean things, but somehow, they were still able to reframe them from the perspective of seeing the negative event that happened as being done *for* them. As a result, they end up stronger and smarter in spite of events or actions from which many others *never* recovered.

"A setback is a setup for a comeback" is an oft-quoted phrase credited to Bishop T.D. Jakes. If your attitude is that your legacy is beyond repair, you are probably right. However, if your current legacy is nowhere near what you would like for it to be, but you still have the bandwidth to picture a legacy that is nothing short of amazing *and* you believe it's never too late to turn it around, then I say again, you're probably right. If you want a masterpiece and are willing to start fresh today, I'd say you're the type of person who will end up leaving a stellar legacy. Comebacks are what motivating stories are made of, whether in family, business, or sports.

Some of the greatest, most memorable moments in history seem to come on the heels of something that went woefully wrong. The common denominator is that the person or persons involved never gave up. They honestly believed the situation could be turned around. They didn't throw in the proverbial towel, never to be heard of again. Some of the best examples of this, and some of the easiest to highlight, are from the world of sports.

For example, one of the greatest moments in golf of all time came in 2005 on hole number 16 of The Masters Tournament. Tiger Woods had just hit one of his poorer shots of the tournament and left everyone hoping for an opportunity for par. Because of his errant shot, Woods found himself in a very bad place on the 16th hole. In spite of this, Woods' next shot was arguably one of the best shots of his career and one of the best shots in Masters history. Miraculously, he made the thirty-foot chip on a heavily slanted green to make a birdie. That shot landed him in a two-way tie at the end of the tournament which forced a sudden death extra hole. On the first hole of sudden death, Woods made a fifteen-foot birdie putt to win the tournament. But what he did on the sixteenth hole ultimately earned him the opportunity to win the 2005 Masters Tournament. It was what he did *after* he found himself in a very bad place that earned him his fourth Masters Championship.

When you find yourself in a bad place, what do you do? Too

many tend to throw in the towel too early and maybe make an excuse, "Well, I tried." They play their victim card. Others, tend to double down and envision a path out of the bad place in which you find yourselves. If you find yourself in a bad place regarding the legacy you would like to leave to, and for, your heirs, now is the time to double down and re-establish the vision for your legacy. It's rarely too late to have a fresh start to create something truly special!

There is never a bad time to start focusing on the future you would like to have for yourself and your family. Likewise, there is never a bad time to think about the type of legacy you would like to leave to future generations. For some, it's only after realizing how their current legacy is shaping up that the decision is made to do things differently. For others, they have been in proximity with others who are already focusing on their legacy. This makes it much easier for them to get ahead of the curve and have a generational consciousness from a much earlier age.

Handling a failure or setback well gives us wisdom through experience, for a bigger, brighter, better future. Handled poorly, however, that same event can cause us to retreat so far that we forever hide our gift that was meant to add significant value to the world. So, adopt the adage, "Things are done for me, not to me."

> *"You cannot consistently perform in a manner which is inconsistent with the way you see yourself."*
>
> – Zig Ziglar

Let's review some common frameworks we use in the coaching and leadership world to help individuals fight back from shortcomings and hit their targets. Too often, the majority of those I've worked with over the years have taken more of a shotgun approach to hitting targets. The biggest reason for this is that the targets weren't really their own. They tended to rely on the whims or expectations of others, whether at a corporate level or a personal level, to even identify a target. When there is no real buy-in for the target, it's very difficult to be consistent with the behaviors necessary to hit said targets.

In my experience, the concept of reverse engineering is one of the best ways to make sure a target is hit and oftentimes even exceeded. Even when there is no real buy-in for the target, reverse engineering is a fantastic strategy. It starts with the end in mind and works backward. In other words, it requires at least a little effort to think about what you'd like the end to look like. Some say getting the mental picture is the number one motivation for implementing a strategy. Unfortunately, too many feel the effort required to get that picture is too time-consuming, too inconvenient or too challenging to create a picture. But once you have it, *then* you will be able to work from the end all the way back to present-day with possible next steps.

Just the very process of coming up with possible next steps is the very process necessary to reach a particular end picture. It also allows for an increased level of energy to see the process to completion. Energy allows the person or persons involved in the process to stick with something long enough to begin seeing a pathway to getting to their target! I mentioned it earlier but it's worth mentioning again, if there is no buy-in, no emotional engagement in hitting the target, or when things get tough, challenging or simply too inconvenient, the necessary behaviors begin to disappear. And we all know by now that anything worthwhile will *always* be met with countless obstacles.

Missing a key behavior once isn't the end of the world, nor does it make the ability to hit the target impossible. But one miss will usually turn into a second miss, and then a third, and so on. Once we miss it just once, it's incredibly easy to miss it again and again. A consistent pattern is how habits begin to form. And before you know it, you aren't doing it at all. My mentor, John

Maxwell, has a phrase that really fits here. He says it this way: Consistency Compounds.

The concept of consistency compounds is a double-edged sword. When the habits and behaviors are positive, this type of consistency works *for* us. But when the habits and behaviors are negative, they work against us. In other words, when we begin to miss a key behavior multiple times, we are consistent in a negative way. The negative consistency serves only to reinforce a negative behavior. It's a basic human pattern. Before you know it, we begin to consistently miss doing the very things that could have gotten us to where we want to go.

Fortunately, the opposite is also true. When we begin to string along multiple days of doing what we set out to do, doing it another day becomes more likely. Consistency is a momentum builder in either direction. Even when we don't have a significant personal and emotional buy-in to something, the very fact that we've been doing something on a consistent basis is empowering enough to keep doing it. So without the buy-in, we rely on pure discipline and willpower. *With* proper buy-in, we can also lean on passion, in addition to following the process for a desired outcome, to help fuel us to reach the stated outcome.

Chapter Application

Reflection:

- Failure should be viewed as a precursor to success.
- View the negative things that have happened in your life as being done *for* you and not *to* you. This negates a victim mentality.
- "A setback is a setup for a comeback." - Bishop T.D. Jakes

Implementation:

- Intentionally reframe every negative thing in your life as being done *for* you. Take time to write out "XYZ was done *for* me to be able to grow..."
- From your ideal legacy, begin to reverse engineer the behaviors necessary to make it a reality.

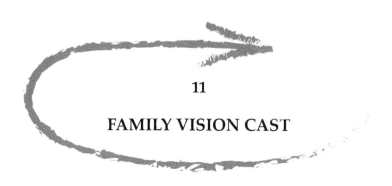

11

FAMILY VISION CAST

"Leaders have three fundamental responsibilities: They craft a vision, they build alignment, and they champion execution."

– Anonymous

IF YOU HAVE A TITLE, whether you're a founder or owner, a C-Suite leader, a line worker, or a parent, you can dictate things get done within your own family. Granted, you may not act like a dictator, but because of your positional authority, your instruction carries a tremendous amount of weight. When you arrive at home, you may still be very comfortable with giving clear direction on getting certain things done. However, you can't fire a family member. So, your approach will be better received with a softer, more relational touch.

We will dig into the various ways a family can 1) get crystal clear on what their family legacy will be to cast vision; 2) gain buy-in through communication, mindset, relationships, and an overall identity consistent with having multi-generational impact; and 3) execute by reviewing some step-by-step actions that will greatly impact the likelihood of your desired legacy being realized. For the remainder of the book, I'll share a variety of ways to excel at all three of these.

For the vast majority of those I work with, they feel creating and casting vision, creating buy-in and alignment, and following through with execution at home is much harder than completing the same tasks in their career fields. This is the real motivation behind this book: to equip others with tools to identify and create a legacy literally worth dying for!

CREATING YOUR OWN ANNUAL FAMILY VISION CAST

"Vision is a destination - a fixed point to which we focus all effort. Strategy is a route - an adaptable path to get us where we want to go."

– Simon Sinek

Without a doubt, starting our family's Annual Family Vision Cast was the single biggest component for long-term change. When we did the very first version of this, my boys were around 14, 11, and nine. Our nine-year-old was really not old enough to fully understand goal setting. But he was all over the part where we started talking about possible family vacations for the upcoming year.

Our first attempt at this was a very simple one-pager with just a handful of questions. The last year we did it all together as a family, a decade later, that one-pager had turned into a multi-page booklet. There were approximately 15 pages. We rented a cabin in Gatlinburg, Tennessee, for a three-day weekend. The booklet had a cover page with a picture of the cabin and the amazing view it had of the Smoky Mountains. We even included a table of contents. That last year we had a couple of young ladies join with our sons, so we added a couple of gender-based breakouts we creatively named His & Hers.

Before I get into the framework, let's briefly dissect the quote at the beginning of this chapter. To begin to create your own family identity, you must be clear on what you stand for, as an individual *and* as a family. Only then does it make any sense to begin thinking about a strategy. A strategy-first mentality is the typical pattern of the impatient. A strategy-first approach may very well put you on the path that someone else created that looks satisfactory, but it is *not* fully yours. This is a great way to get you effectively and efficiently headed in a direction that isn't really you. So, set the vision first.

The vision may be best viewed as a top-down driven approach if your family consists mainly of younger children. What does a five-year-old know about what they want to accomplish over the next twelve months, let alone be able to contribute to the family vision? However, at some point, the most effective approach will be to include the older children to foster buy-in. Conducting your own annual family vision cast is an activity that can be family-driven for many, many years.

What follows is the actual template I've shared with clients for nearly twenty years to initiate their own family vision cast. It has been greatly modified from the first one all those years ago. Yours can be as in-depth or as simple as you desire. The real purpose is to begin creating an intentional, repeatable pattern that literally turns into part of your legacy. Over time, your kids will begin to look forward to these little family retreats. Further, you will be laying the groundwork to transfer an amazing blessing of family vision and values.

WHY & HOW TO CREATE AN ANNUAL FAMILY VISION CAST

The Annual Family Vision Cast is designed to be a resource for you to be more intentional with your family. But it's especially for your kids to be better equipped to tackle the world than you were. So, if you're serious about laying the groundwork to equip your family and take the first step toward your intentional legacy, let's get started!

1. THE PURPOSE

What is an Annual Family Vision Cast? It's a fun time to get the entire family engaged in creating a bigger, brighter, more enjoyable existence as a family, both now and in the future. It's an opportunity to create a new and healthy family tradition by creating living memories (I'll explain what those are soon), creating brighter futures, and resourcing your kids with tools they'll use well after they leave the shelter of your home. Finally, defining and communicating why this is important to do as a family is vital.

Determining what you expect to accomplish from hosting your own Annual Family Vision Cast and defining why you are doing it is like an accelerant that can fan into flame your best lives as a family. When an emotion is tied to your vision (plans), you will feel as if the vision is pulling you forward and not you pushing to make something happen.

Your Annual Family Vision Cast is an intentional time, typically towards the end of the year *or* at the very beginning of the new year, to review the highlights and lessons of the previous year, as well as to create a vision with positive expectations for the coming year. Notice the word choice of "lessons." Be intentional about how you frame things that didn't go well or not as well as expected. Notice I didn't say "review the setbacks or what went wrong." Instead, I choose to view things like that as lessons. Our choice of words will create an area of focus. If you focus on what went wrong as opposed to what lessons you learned, you will tend to have a negative view on something that could be positive. You cannot have a vision for a bigger, brighter, more enjoyable future with a negative frame of mind.

I personally encourage you to include children ages 10 and up in this process...obviously manage your expectations, knowing their attention span is most likely much shorter than yours.

Over time, your Annual Family Vision Cast will likely become *the* constant you will be able to point to as *the one thing* that prepared your family for its greatest level of success. It helps marriages get and remain on the same page (or at least within the same book), and it will equip your children with tools and resources to help them successfully launch out on their own to eventually create their individual year-end review traditions with their own families.

You may be wondering why this matters. This part is *huge*. Without a compelling why, even little challenges will become too much. This new tradition improves internal family relationships, opens up ongoing lines of communication, strengthens each family member's ability to think critically and strategically, and prepares everyone for a bigger, brighter, more enjoyable future.

Your Annual Family Vision Cast will pay dividends for decades and hopefully even centuries to come. It *will* outlive you! For those with a legacy mindset, this equips you with a formal platform to begin to instill, and solidify year after year, those principles that matter most to you. When the time comes for your kids to leave your home and go out on their own, the things they'll take with them are mostly those things lived out and not just talked about.

"Failed plans should not be interpreted as a failed vision. Visions don't change, they are only refined. Plans rarely stay the same and are scrapped or adjusted as needed. Be stubborn about the vision, but flexible with your plan."

– John C. Maxwell

2. THE CATEGORIES

This is the creative part of the process. Which categories you ultimately choose in your Family Vision Plan is personal to you. You can be very structured or more fluid. You can keep it simple and do it at a local coffee shop, a hotel atrium, or you can schedule a family getaway in a cabin somewhere. The goal is to be creative, keep it fun, and get it on the calendar!

Dr. Nick Howard puts it this way, "Essentially, vision work is about prayerfully developing or imagining ideal scenarios in the areas of your life that are the most important to you, that fill your heart with hope and energy and focus and perhaps wonder."

CATEGORY OPTIONS, IDEAS, STRUCTURE OR FORMAT:

Here you get to personalize what you choose to discuss during your own Annual Family Vision Cast. You can make it as simple or elaborate as you like. Below are some possible ways to create your own categories to discuss:

- Reflect & Plan: This is two parts - spend some time reviewing the past year, as well as dreaming into the upcoming year.
- The 7-F's: Faith, Family, Fun, Finances, Fitness, Fellowship, Filanthropic (yes, I know it is spelled with a P - but I like 7-F's better than just 6-F's)
- Marriage, Parenting, Kids, Health, Entertainment/Travel/Leisure, Career

Feel free to use any combination of the above or create your own - this will likely be altered year after year.

3. THE PROCESS

The easiest format is to simply break this exercise into two parts: Reflect (past) & Plan (future). In Reflect, you look back over the last calendar year and simply ask questions like:

- What were the highlights? (vacations, accomplishments, celebrations, etc)
- What were some of the lessons learned from last year?
- What should be repeated/what can be improved?

In the "Plan" part, you look into the upcoming year and ask questions like:

- What do you want to accomplish next year?
- What do we want to do as a family?
- Vacations? Let each member throw out ideas. Then ask, "What would you enjoy about that?" Include the question "why?" often. Get multiple answers and "dream" into each of them. This is the foundation in creating excitement, buy-in and a "Living Memory".
- For adults - what awards, education/degrees/certifications, promotions, new business(es)
- For kids - what grades, sports accolades, turning a certain age, etc.

Get input from each family member. The goal is to keep it fun, NOT tyrannical.

The beautiful thing about living memories is they are something that can be enjoyed an unlimited number of times. The first phase begins when first asking, "What would you like to do and what would you enjoy about it?" It creates excitement *and* builds new neural pathways because it engages the imagination.

The second phase begins when you actually experience the event, vacation, or activity. And finally, the never-ending phase is in remembering and talking about the event, vacation, or activity countless times *after* it's over. Some of our strongest positive memories are those where we intentionally went through this exercise–knowingly and intentionally creating a living memory.

*You may want to use some of the other categories and also break those into past & future focus, *or* just use one of the other categories when looking into the upcoming year. It's your plan, so it's your call.

Once you complete this exercise, you will have done what well over 90% of families will never do. Honestly, this is likely one of the more important exercises you can complete together as a family. It's your future and your kids' future we are talking about, so this is *not* the place to consider cutting corners!

FAMILY RULES TO LIVE BY

At the end of your Vision Cast document, list out your top four, five, ten, or twelve core values as a couple and as a family. What are your absolutes? What principles guide the way you live and interact with humanity as individuals and as a family? How will your family name be remembered? These "rules" are to be treated as if they are laws. When implemented, they will often act as a decision-maker on your behalf. Write them out and include them at the end. (Examples: We will always tell the truth; We will not gossip; We will help others in need; As a family, we have each other's backs; As a family, we know there is a solution to every challenge; We see every challenge as an opportunity; We will abc; We will not xyz; etc.)

IMPACTFUL QUOTES & BIBLE VERSES

Include impactful quotes and/or Bible verses that trigger a

healthy response towards growing into and leaning toward your vision. These can be scattered throughout your document. Place them where the point of the quote fits with that particular section.

4. THE REVIEW

Now that it's completed, what's next? First, I'd ask the others in the family to share at least one thing that really stood out to them in doing the Family Vision Cast. In the business world, we call this a debrief. Then, you can plan to celebrate and commemorate by going out to eat at a nice restaurant. Or you may choose to make a favorite meal and special dessert at home. Be mindful to create a memory. Finally, determine that you, as parents, will review this at least quarterly to assess how things are going in the new year.

CHAPTER APPLICATION

Reflection:

- There are four key parts in facilitating your family vision cast: The Purpose, The Categories, The Process, and The Review.
- Creating family vision is the responsibility of parents.

Implementation:

- Review numbers 1-4 again and get your family vision cast on the calendar.
- Craft a vision, build alignment, and champion execution.

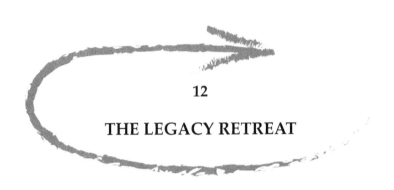

12

THE LEGACY RETREAT

"Legacy is not leaving something for people. It's leaving
something in people."

– Peter Strople

AS WE ADDRESSED AT THE very beginning of the book, leaving
a financial inheritance is only one leg of the Legacy Table. The
financial piece of what you leave behind will only last *when* the
other three legs of the table are adequately addressed. The legacy
retreat is an intentional approach to perpetuating your vision,
values, knowledge, and wealth indefinitely. The Legacy retreat is
for laying the groundwork for multiple generations to come,
ideally indefinitely. And indefinitely is an incredibly long time.

This cannot happen when you simply set up some sophisti-
cated legal documents and powerful wealth-creation vehicles.
Those documents and financial vehicles are part of it, but only
focusing on legal vehicles will fall a good bit short of the target
of lasting indefinitely. As previously stated, statistically your
wealth will *not* make it beyond the next couple of generations.
The answer to this dilemma is *not* more legal documents to

restrict access to wealth. The answer is intentionally getting all of your family members on the same page as quickly as possible, then reviewing and adjusting the vision and tactics annually from here on out regarding the Vision, Values, Knowledge, and Wealth strategies. Anything less will leave the confidence of any particular legacy up in the air.

What follows is what I call **The Legacy Retreat**. It is intended to be an annual event where you facilitate an intentional discussion of the four pillars of perpetuating a highly intentional legacy that discusses the transfer of: Vision, Values, Knowledge, Wealth. This guide is meant to equip, empower, and encourage you in doing your next, or your first, Legacy Retreat. Depending on the expanse of your current estate (multiple businesses, multiple verticals, etc.), this could be a multi-day event. Remember that family mentioned at the beginning of this book? Their "event" covered the span of several weeks! If this is something you would like support with, please reach out to me through our website: *thelancewelch.com*.

For your first Legacy Retreat, I would recommend using the template provided below. After you have done your own event a couple of times, you will then want to customize your retreat to make sure it specifically meets your desired targets.

What follows is an example or format for you to follow. There will be sample uses of verbiage as well.

SECTIONS

- Purpose *(Define your purpose or your desired outcome)*
- Agenda/Table of Contents:

  Master Legacy Statement
  Transfer of Vision
  Transfer of Values
  Transfer of Knowledge

Transfer of Wealth
Annual Vision Cast & Legacy Retreat

- Format *(Is it hours or days for your own legacy retreat? Is it held in a private or public location?)*
- Retreat Discussion Guide Outline *(This is a handout.)*

PURPOSE

The Legacy Retreat is intended to be an annual event where we facilitate an intentional discussion of the four legs of the legacy table to perpetuate the legacy of our choosing: Vision - Values - Knowledge - Wealth. This workshop guide is to equip, empower and encourage us in doing our first retreat.

Remember, in the event you'd like some support at your family retreat(s), that can be arranged by contacting the author.

AGENDA

- **Master Legacy Statement**

Create a legacy theme, in two to four sentences, that encapsulates the who, what, and why for you and your family name. Next, create an overall legacy statement that lists several categories that matter to you, such as what you want your name connected to or aligned with specific passions. This could be wealth-based, faith-based, philanthropy-based, values-based, impact-based, or a combination of multiple things that are all condensed down to one page or less. For example, you might research your family crest, family history, and even create your own. *Examples of topics for your Legacy Statement are at the end of this chapter.*

- **Transfer of Vision**

We know that "where there is no vision, the people perish." What this simply means is that without clarity on where you want your family legacy to be, the chances it will actually look even remotely close to the target is very slim.

- **Transfer of Values**

This includes the meaning of your family name, family values, and family vision statement. Make sure to create or download that family crest to tie it all together. I would suggest that all members have input for ownership and buy-in, keeping it age-appropriate.

- **Transfer of Knowledge**

This part includes intellectual capital, industry specific advantages, business philosophies, generational wisdom, and specific "how-to" strategies.

- **Transfer of Wealth**

This encompasses current asset allocations, wealth transfer vehicles, transfer strategies, various legal entities, legal and tax document reviews, etc.

- **Annual Review**

This includes review of business(es), current and forecast data and trends, tax and trust strategies, family net worth, philanthropic activities, goals and targets.

FORMAT FOR YOUR OWN RETREAT

Create a packet, typically four to eight pages per business or a vertical (additional pages if you include financial statements)

- Who to include:

    Immediate and extended family
    Key advisors - for their portion only

- New and old wealth review

    Businesses, real estate, precious metals, art,
        patents, etc.

- Time allotted (number of hours or days)

    Simple version in as little as half a day per
        business
    Multiple businesses may be one to three
        days per entity

- Ideal locations

    Family vacation property
    Resorts
    All-inclusives

ANNUAL LEGACY RETREAT

This activity is more than the normal annual business projections. This is taking pride in the family name and *all* that it stands for. A family name is known for something regardless of what's going on in the marketplace. Create pride in the name for your younger family members. Use the following five bullets to create your own personal family legacy statement(s):

- Who are we (identity)
- Where are we headed (vision transfer)
- What we stand for (values transfer)
- How we are able to impact future generations (specialized knowledge transfer)
- The extent that will we impact future generations (wealth/vision/values transfer)

*This must be communicated and re-communicated year after year - NEVER skipped - you cannot assume it will be remembered from the previous year.

To help you get started in creating your own legacy statements, I have provided 18 different examples for you at the end of this book in Appendix D.

The typical precursor to the Legacy Retreat is hosting your own Annual Family Vision Cast as discussed in the previous chapter, but not always. For example, our focus with the Family Vision Cast was primarily on equipping our kids to do, be, and have more than us and to know how to think, plan, and set goals for themselves. It has a shorter scope of focus as well. It only looks back over the last year and forward into the next year from a mainly personal perspective (not business). The Family Vision Cast is certainly more lighthearted and geared towards families with kids still at home.

The Legacy Retreat has a focus that is typically better suited for high-net-worth families with multiple businesses being run by family members and include multiple generations at the retreat. It will be run more like a multi-day business meeting. This retreat type format allows for intentional discussions regarding the transfer of all four legs of the legacy table while also creating formal training opportunities to not only hang on to family wealth but also how to keep creating more of it.

While any family can facilitate a legacy retreat, it's time to seek the help of a facilitator like myself if the following conditions apply: you want to be intentional regarding your legacy, you have multiple businesses, you have family members and multiple generations in those businesses, and you have a net worth north of $5 million (but especially if over $10 million). If that is of interest to you, please contact me directly through my website: thelancewelch.com.

CHAPTER APPLICATION

Reflection:

- The biggest difference between the Legacy Retreat and the Family Vision Cast is the length of time for which we focus on it.
- The Legacy Retreat is ideally suited for high-net-worth families with multiple businesses *or* children involved in the family business.
- Your Legacy Retreat *is* an annual event and should not be skipped.

Implementation:

- Determine if a Family Vision Cast or a Family Legacy Retreat is better suited for your present situation.
- Consider bringing in a facilitator for at least the first retreat to get the most out of it.

13

LEAVING WELL-PREPARED

"Man appears for a little while to laugh and weep, to work and play, and then to go to make room for those who shall follow him in the never-ending cycle."

– A. W. Tozer

WHEN IT COMES TO PLANNING for the inevitable, Benjamin Franklin's is one phrase I heard likely more than any other throughout my career. That phrase is, "In this world nothing can be said to be certain, except death and taxes." I guess it was an attempt at putting a slightly lighter spin on a sometimes heavy subject, which is death. I get it, planning for the inevitable is inconvenient. But not planning ahead *will* prove even more inconvenient later.

The interesting thing about leaving this life well is that the majority of the time, you won't know when that time will be. I often hear it said of a young person who passes away that it was untimely. I don't know about you, but when that time comes for me, those closest to me will likely all consider it untimely.

There are literally countless ways in which to make sure you have your affairs in order long before you think they are needed. This is true whether you're talking about the highly complicated estate planning and business succession strategy for multiple businesses or the most basic of life insurance plans for final expenses. The point at which it is needed most will be too late to implement any of the plans, hopes or dreams to make this transition smoother and significant for the next generation.

Allow me to share some real life examples, both the good and the not so good. Remember, this is *not* deemed as advice for estate planning, taxes, insurance, or anything else requiring a license to do so.

THE GOOD:

Family A had a very successful business (textiles and manufacturing) and four kids, two of which were active in the business. They met with their team of advisors to discuss not only their potential estate tax dilemma, but also how to possibly structure an estate plan that didn't accidentally favor the two kids active in the business. You see, absent intentional planning, it would have been very feasible to inadvertently see a scenario where the two kids *in* the business could have inherited the business, along with the vast majority of the family wealth and the other two kids get the crumbs of the business.

Or another possible scenario would have been where the two children with *no* knowledge of the manufacturing business became equal owners with the two who knew everything about the industry. In this situation, you would have two with all of the responsibilities sharing everything equally with those with no responsibilities. This wouldn't play out well in the long term.

We used a method called an Estate Equalization Strategy. It was just that–a strategy that used a combination of life insurance and specific legal documents to get it all set up. It was not a product or something tied to a particular tax code. The result was a strategy that was pretty equal in how the family business and net worth were allocated at death. And the best part was that since this was established well in advance of any death occurring, there were built-in formulas to help pre-determine valuations and familial splits whether something happened relatively soon or many years in the future. It took a tremendous amount of pressure off the parents who ultimately built everything.

In this scenario, there was never any animosity amongst the kids because of a perceived favorable treatment of those active in the business versus those not in the business or vice versa. Another beneficial part of this particular example was the level of transparency from the patriarchs to all four of their children. The heirs were not only kept in the loop about the intent of the planning but were also consulted along the way. Checklists were provided for both the planning phase as well as a checklist for survivors after a death. See Appendix E for similar checklists.

THE NOT-SO-GOOD:

Family B owned a lot of land, which included some pasture and some timber. The family had visited with planners in the past but decided it was too expensive to implement any of the suggestions that were from highly-qualified professionals. Yes, I was one of those highly-qualified professionals. Their plan wasn't inexpensive but it wasn't cheap, either. For them to do everything they professed they wanted would have run well into the six-figures. (But as you'll see, that was cheap compared to the cost of doing nothing.)

Fast forward a couple of years, and the parents, both in their mid-sixties, were killed in a car wreck. At the time, the estate tax rate was fifty percent and the estate tax bill was due within nine months from the date of death.

Here is where things started getting dicey. Since there was no formal estate plan in place, the IRS had no alleged valuation to go by, so they assigned one on their own. Unfortunately for the family, the IRS assigned the valuation based on the hundreds of acres of timber. The category of timber was significantly more valuable than simply assigning it a value based on the agriculture category. There were plenty of examples, or a precedence, of the IRS using a pre-established valuation of families that had entered into an objective estate planning structure before death. While there was no hard and fast rule in place for them to do so, the IRS often would go with prior appraisals or estimates and allow the previous work to stand as long as there appeared to be proper due diligence.

In this situation, the family was provided a tax bill in excess of $7 million, due within nine months of death. But again, unfortunately for the family, it took the IRS over five months to provide the settlement amount. This meant the family had just over three months to come up with the cash. And guess what? They didn't have nearly that amount of cash. They were asset-rich and cash-strapped, which means they were definitely not cash poor, but certainly not sitting on enough cash to cover the tax bill.

While there were options available in getting the IRS paid, those options looked like taking the IRS on as a business partner. And who wants that? So, the family felt their only real option was to begin selling off land to come up with the additional cash. Again, unfortunately for the family, to sell large amounts of very expensive land typically requires much longer than a few months. They ended up selling the land at a deep discount to attract the deeper pockets of buyers that could buy, close, and fund in the timeframe needed. If I recall correctly, they ended up selling close to $9 million worth of land to actually come up with enough cash to settle and clear their estate tax bill.

On a positive note for this family, with the exception of their lack of estate planning implementation, they were very well-prepared for the two kids to step in and take over every aspect of running this large agricultural business. The kids' names were clearly added to all necessary deeds, assets, and liabilities of the organization years before they would have been needed. They knew where all vendor and creditor information was stored. They were added on to all articles of incorporation, legal documents, and checking accounts. They did so much right. But where they dropped the ball was in the timely execution of wealth preservation strategies and it cost the next generation millions upon millions of dollars.

There were countless times I received a call from someone I'd never met asking if their parents had purchased any life insurance from me because they'd found my business card somewhere in the piles of information they were rummaging through. The vast majority of the time, the answer was, "No, I'm sorry, they chose not to take any insurance out." In these situations, their parents had passed away and hadn't done anything to get their affairs in order. The kids, while still dealing with extreme grief, were put in a position to simply start digging through laundry baskets full of information. They didn't know if there was any life insurance. Or, other times the kids felt there was insurance in place but had no idea which company held the policy, let alone have an actual policy number or point of contact.

Only after going through the piles of stuff, were they able to identify the name of the bank with which their parents worked. Then once they contacted the bank, they learned none of the kids were included on any of the accounts. As such, they couldn't get information on the mortgage to make payments or keep the utilities on. And what about any pets of the deceased? These all sound like simple things to address until it's sprung on you at a very stressful, trying time when you'd rather not be having to deal with any of these things.

Here are some additional things to check on:

- What about advance care directives?
- Is there a last will & testament?
- Do you have a living will?
- What about a Do Not Resuscitate (DNR)?

These may all seem like really heavy things to talk about, and they are. Again, having this conversation may be very inconvenient right now but it *will* prove significantly more inconvenient later if these types of conversations never take place.

As we come to the end of this chapter, what conclusions have you come to? What are some areas you recognize should be addressed sooner than later? I have yet to see a time where choosing *not* to have these hard discussions turned out to be a good idea. It's not enough for you to say, "Yeah, Lance, I need to look into this." From decades of working with people, when someone starts out a phrase with "I *need* to...", I honestly get a little sad because the word "need" is not a word that signifies anything will actually get done.

Again, this is my own personal experience. It's like someone saying, "I need to lose weight." Then they usually don't. But if they were to say, "I am going to lose weight," I believe them. The phrase that starts with "I am" is a power phrase that indicates true change *is* expected. So, you can say, "I am going to set up an appointment to begin addressing some of these concerns." And I get it. Sometimes there is a hindrance to someone being comfortable using an "I am" statement because they honestly don't know where to start.

So, I want to help you not be one of those families that allow good intentions to lead nowhere. I want better for you than putting your heirs in the position of sifting through drawers or laundry baskets of information looking for things that can honestly be addressed with a little time and forethought. In the

Appendices, I've added some checklists to help you with these very important conversations with aging parents, as well as for you to dig into this type of preparation for your own peace of mind.

CHAPTER APPLICATION

Reflection:

- There is no shortage of creative ways to make sure you've done all the planning necessary to ensure your heirs are well prepared to settle your estate.
- Work with experienced planning professionals to identify exactly how you would like your estate to work with and for your heirs.

Implementation:

- Review or create your last will and testament.
- Review Appendix E and complete prior to meeting with planning professionals.
- Become familiar with terms such as advanced directives, DNR, and living will.

14

CONCLUSION

"Vision without action is merely a dream. Action without vision just passes the time. Vision with action can change the world."

– Joel Barker

WHERE ARE YOU IN THE "legacy navigating" process? What are your intentions now that you've finished this resource? It was Bernard of Clairvaux who said, "The road to hell is paved with good intentions." I understand that his intent was to incite action over just an intention. But ALL action starts first as an intention or as a thought. I want to encourage you to take at least a little time to consider your next steps. Then, ideally, get the first step on your calendar.

When I was younger, I was told that leaders were readers. So I decided to become a voracious reader. I set goals for myself to read 50+ books a year. And for many years I did just that. Even though I consumed an amazing amount of data on leadership, sales, fatherhood, and marriage, my focus was more on hitting my reading goal and less on any intentional application of the data I was reading about. Fortunately, a lot of the information I was acquiring did get put into practice but I can't help but wonder, what would've happened if I would have been more focused on the implementation and execution of all of those resources?

So again, where are you in the process?

Many people who are serious about leveling up their family legacy are already doing quite well in one or two of the legacy legs but could afford to increase their focus on the other legs. So, on which leg are you currently the strongest? The Vision Leg? The Values Leg? The Knowledge Leg? The Wealth Leg? Like just about every area of your life, your awareness will drive your next steps. Since you can't address what you are not aware of, what are you now aware of that creates what is going to be next for you and your family?

It is at this point I offer you an opportunity to become highly intentional about creating the legacy of your wildest dreams and quite literally, to change the trajectory of your family name. It was Benjamin Franklin who said, "To succeed, jump as quickly at opportunities as you do at conclusions."

Are you familiar with the phrase "Call to Action"? This is also known as a CTA. Don't worry, I'm not asking for your information or your credit card! Simply put, a call to action is encouraging someone to make a decision to do something differently than before. Oftentimes, the CTA is associated with a big discount if you "buy now." Other times, the CTA is associated with low inventory, creating a Fear Of Missing Out, or FOMO. In this case, you are encouraged to act fast before the offer is gone. My call to action is to take what you've learned in this book and utilize the resources in the upcoming appendixes to create lasting change for you and ALL of your future generations.

It is my honest, heartfelt determination to make emotional deposits into the lives of my three sons, as well as their spouses and my grandkids, until my own coffin lid closes. Only then am I officially done! I truly believe that when I model a generational consciousness to my immediate family, it will make it highly likely they will do the same for their own respective families. Then they will want to see their heirs be far more successful in every way imaginable than they themselves have been. As my talk and my actions align, I *will* have a generational impact!

As we've discussed, it will likely be inconvenient to start something new right now. But it will be far more inconvenient if you choose to procrastinate on this and have something happen that is irreversible later and you can no longer take the desired action you could take today. Besides, statistics clearly show that if you procrastinate on starting something new, doing it someday will continually get pushed out further and further to the point that it can no longer be done at all.

So, since you've made it all the way to the end of this book, I encourage you to become even more intentional about creating the legacy of your dreams and in doing so, you'll begin changing the world. And if you'd like to get a little help with implementing your first Legacy Retreat, you can go to thelancewelch.com to schedule an initial review.

APPENDIX A: THE CORE VALUES EXERCISE

"Personal leadership is the process of keeping your vision and values before you and aligning your life to be congruent with them."

– Stephen Covey

Your core values are intended to be the springboard that propels you into the other three legs of the Legacy Table. Identifying the top five values probably won't be all that easy. But like everything else we have been discussing, anything worthwhile will be inconvenient. But staying the same is far more inconvenient. I'm hoping you've already learned that lesson, right? You don't get to where you want to be without incurring *and* pressing through inconvenience.

<u>There are three steps to this exercise:</u>
 Step 1: Read through the entire list once to create a frame of reference. Then go back through the list and circle your Top 20 values (or write them on a separate sheet of paper or tablet).

Step 2: In reviewing your Top 20, go through and cut your list in half to identify your Top 10.

Step 3: Finally, in reviewing your Top 10, cut it in half again to identify your Top Five Core Values.

Accountability · Achievement · Acceptance
Accomplishment · Accuracy · Adaptability · Adventure
Alertness · Altruism · Ambition · Assertiveness
Attentive · Authenticity · Awareness · Balance
Beauty · Being the best · Belonging · Bravery
Brilliance · Calm · Candor · Capable · Caring
Challenge · Clear · Clever · Collaboration
Commitment · Common Sense · Communication
Community · Compassion · Competence · Confidence
Connection · Consistent · Contentment · Control
Creative · Courageous · Curious · Dedicated
Dependable · Decisive · Dignity · Disciplined
Diversity · Efficient · Equality · Empathetic
Enthusiastic Ethical · Excellence · Fairness · Faith
Family Fearless · Ferocious · Forgiveness · Formidable
Friendly · Fun · Future Focused · Generous · Giving
Back · Grace · Gratitude · Greatness · Growth
Minded · Harmony · Hard Work · Health · Honesty
Honor · Hope · Humility · Humor · Inclusion
Independence · Initiative · Insightful · Integrity
Intuition · Irreverent · Joy · Kindness · Knowledge
Lawful · Leadership · Leisure · Logic · Love
Loyalty · Mastery · Maturity · Motivation · Nature
Openness · Optimism · Order · Originality · Passion
Patience · Patriotism · Peace · Perseverance
Persistence · Power · Pride · Realistic · Recognition
Reliability · Resourcefulness · Respect
Responsibility · Results-Oriented · Reverence · Risk

Taking · Safety · Security · Self-discipline · Self-expression · Self-respect · Serenity · Service Simplicity · Significance · Skillfulness · Sincerity Smart · Spirituality · Sportsmanship · Status Stewardship · Success · Teamwork · Thankful Thorough · Thoughtful · Thrifty · Tolerance Toughness · Tradition · Tranquility · Transparency Travel · Trust · Truth · Understanding · Uniqueness Unity · Usefulness · Victory · Vigor · Vision Vitality Vulnerability · Warrior · Wealth · Welcoming · Well-being · Whimsical · Wholeheartedness · Winning Wisdom · Wonder

Now that you have your Top Five Core Values, decide how you are going to make them known to the rest of the family. Consider creating a Family Crest using these five core values.

Consider incorporating these five values into your Family Vision Cast or Legacy Retreats. Communicating your core values is not a one and done type of activity. This will be a key contributor to your family legacy *if* and *when* your future decisions are made in light of intentionally aligning your decisions with your values.

APPENDIX B: THINGS I WANT MY KIDS TO BE EQUIPPED TO DO

In this exercise, think back to when you left home for the real world. This is normally either post-high school or post-college. Recall some of the things you wish you had already known how to do. What were some of your key lessons along the way? What are some things you do now that are second nature for you but would not be to someone right out of school?

For now, let's commit to starting a list of at least 10 things you would like your kids to either understand or know how to do prior to leaving home for the real world. Below is a list of thirty possibilities to simply jumpstart your thinking:

- Think for themselves
- Think strategically
- Study the Bible and facilitate their own relationship with God
- Able to forgive others, especially when it's hard
- Ask for and receive forgiveness
- Handling conflict without losing temper
- Importance of good hygiene

- Understanding the importance of solid, healthy friends (inner circle)
- Create a healthy identity separate from their performance
- Count the cost to determine their own acceptable amount of risk
- Be willing and able to learn from any person, regardless of position
- Be intentional to capture and recall a person's name
- See themselves qualified to be in *any* room
- Know how to interact with others of higher authority
- Be an encourager
- Shoot for excellence, not perfection
- Read and understand body language
- Value people's time by not being late
- Mow a lawn
- Change their own tire in an emergency
- Prepare their own meals
- Balance their financial accounts
- Create and stick to a budget
- Read a balance sheet
- Read a profit and loss statement
- Know how to speak in public
- Be able to start their own business
- Be a student of personal growth and leadership
- Understand marriage is hard but well worth it; never quit
- Every decision, or no decision, has a corresponding consequence

APPENDIX C: THE SILVER SWORD AND THE GOLD SWORD

Have you ever heard of the story of the Silver Sword and the Gold Sword?

It's a story of your power and your authority, both personal and professional.

This silver sword is one that we are very, very well trained on how to use, both males and females. But we're trained to use it usually in the professional world. The silver sword represents positional power, a bigger business card, a hierarchy, and positional authority.

It is used to make the tough decisions, to make abrupt decisions. But the silver sword has some downsides to it. A lot of the time, the silver sword is used by people who are not too worried about relationships. This style is more concerned with getting things done at any cost. Granted, there's a place for the silver sword at certain times.

The silver sword is something I always pictured being made out of a surgical stainless steel. It is very, very hard. It can be honed to a razor-sharp edge and it will hold its edge for a very long time. As in the days when swords were used in battle, they were very effective as either an offensive or defensive tool. But when swung wildly, they also had a high likelihood of collateral damage.

If you use the silver sword exclusively in your business, you will find that yes, you can get things done. But you've created a culture most likely that is based on fear and submission.

From my many years in the corporate world, I witnessed it being used time and time again to get quick results to help people climb the ranks of the corporate ladder. And once promoted, there were plenty of damaged relationships left in their wakes.

When those in charge are heavy users of the silver sword, you primarily have an organization or a division of doers, not thinkers. You probably have an organization that is dealing with more turnover than necessary.

Now let's contrast that with the gold sword. The gold sword is a much, much softer metal. Mathematically however, it is much, much, much more valuable. It is of such greater worth, that when you wield the gold sword, you can't just go through the office swinging it around left and right because it will devalue the worth of the metal.

If one handles the gold sword in the same manner as the silver sword, you have chunks of the metal missing. You could even break it and decrease the value of it even more. The more you swing the gold sword in a way so as not to diminish its physical value, the more intentional you are about improving the value of relationships.

Those who are mastering the gold sword create a company culture with less turnover, a team willing to go all in for leadership, and able to be thinkers in addition to being doers.

When asked which sword is best, I say it's not either/or but and/both. The circumstances will dictate which sword is best in any given situation.

Use the silver sword. When necessary, use the gold sword more intentionally.

This is how the Silver Sword and Gold Sword analogy applies in the business world.

What does it look like in one's personal life? In reality, it's very, very similar. Using the silver sword at home is done with little to no intentional concern about the relationship. They may think they are concerned about the relationships in their home, but it's simply not true.

So let's say I bring the silver sword into my home. I've been swinging the silver sword all day and I'm ready to walk into the house and keep on swinging it. I walk through the door and start barking orders and start using the Silver Sword philosophy in the house.

And in many cases, you'll notice that your spouse has a silver sword *and* is also prepared to use it.

Think about the culture that's been created in your own home by solely using the silver sword. You'll likely be met with the other person using their own silver sword. But when you choose to use the gold sword at home, you'll be met with the other person's gold sword as well.

So here is what I learned as a younger leader and relatively newer husband:

Before I walked through the house door, I would mentally and physically go through the motion of taking the silver sword off my belt, hanging it up on a peg that was right there beside my garage door. Then I would pull the gold sword off of the peg on the wall and I would strap it on to my waist. I would actually go through the whole motion of taking the silver sword off and putting the gold sword on. This intentional act allowed me to walk into the house with the gold sword strapped on with a totally different mentality. The more challenging the day, the more intentional I had to be to switch out the swords before entering the house.

As was expected, when I intentionally walked into the house with the gold sword, I was usually met with my spouse carrying her own gold sword. And on those occasions where she'd had a particularly challenging day and was still carrying her silver sword, once she recognized I had the gold sword strapped onto my waist, it was then much easier for her to switch swords also.

APPENDIX D: SAMPLE LEGACY STATEMENTS

My Principles:

__Integrity__: In all I do, I endeavor to act in the best interest of all parties involved and exercise integrity with my personal and business dealings.

__Being a Giver__: I give of myself first in any new relationship and operate under the assumption that the other person is a giver until experience proves otherwise. I forgive others for their mistakes and try to understand things from their point of view.

__Positive Thinking/Speaking__: I focus on the positive attributes of others. When I speak to or about another person, I never say something for the sole purpose of hurting them or blemishing their reputation.

__Responsibility__: I do not blame outside circumstances or others for my mistakes or problems. When something bad happens, I see the role I played and admit to my part. I also treat others' possessions and public spaces as if they were my own and exercise the same kind of care. I don't expect others to clean up after me or take care of my needs.

__Humility__: Everyone has their own brand of intelligence. Everyone fights a battle. I am not better than others. There is *always something to learn from those around me. Sometimes I'm on top, sometimes I'm at rock bottom, sometimes I act smart, sometimes I act like an idiot—just like everyone else does.*

Order: *I keep my life simple, free from clutter, disorder, and things that steal my energy for negative purposes (e.g., addictions, gossip, worry, trivial concerns).*

Curiosity: *I am open to all kinds of outcomes. When things don't go my way, I act as a third-party observer and try to see my situation from a state of curiosity rather than disappointment.*

Action in Spite of Discomfort: *When I know something is right, I immediately take action, even if it's hard or causes short-term discomfort.*

Self-Compassion: *When I make mistakes, I forgive myself and have compassion for my shortcomings. I create an environment for myself that is safe, healthy, and caring. When I need help, I ask for it.*

Fun/Adventure: *Life should be passionate and engaging. I see the wondrous every day. The ordinary becomes extraordinary to me because of how I love, who I interact with, and the joy of my pursuits.*

Nourishing My Soul: *Throughout the day, I take breaks to recharge myself. These include running, working out, spending time in nature, meditation, baths, painting, writing for fun, or reading. I spend several hours a week thinking about ways to improve my character and learning about new concepts and ideas.*

Family Role: *My purpose in my family is to support my family members in their dreams, have fun with them, create lasting memories, be open and truthful, and be a good example.*

I will conduct myself in family life in a manner that enriches our home by my presence. My family will be happy when I'm home. I will be a leader to my extended family

Social Role: *I focus on finding and cultivating deep friendships with people who have similar values and whom I admire and trust.*

Career Role: *I am responsible and pay my bills but focus on work that energizes me. My vision and calling are more important to me than simply earning a high wage. When working with clients, I endeavor to do what is best for them and, at the very least, do no harm.*

I will influence people with example, in walking my talk, in principle-centered living.

Community Role: *Every year, I review what I'm doing to help others to be sure I'm on track. I make an effort to meet new people from different backgrounds and learn from everyone I come into contact with.*

Legacy Statement: *I hold the following principles: By the Grace of God; Forgiveness; Empowering Others; Growing a Garden of Empowerment; Diversity of Race and Culture Is a Gift; I will sustain life in physical, mental, emotional, and spiritual areas. To forgive myself more, and get on with doing good work.*

My Health: *To the best of my ability and taste tolerance, I eat an unprocessed diet focused on organic vegetables, grass-fed or free range meats and other healthy fats, proteins, organic fruit, and limited carbohydrates. Every day, I move my body and expend enough energy to feel healthy, balanced, and in good shape.*

Sharing My Legacy: *I make an effort to document important life moments as they happen and store this documentation in a safe place. I write letters to those who inspire me either as it happens or once a year when I review the happenings of my life. I make a consistent effort to tell others how grateful I am to have them in my life, and I'm specific about what I appreciate about them.*

APPENDIX E: SURVIVOR CHECKLIST

What to do when a loved one dies: A survivor's checklist.

<u>Immediately following the death, you should:</u>
❏ 1. Contact the funeral home to take your loved one into their care.

❏ 2. Contact your minister.

❏ 3. Alert immediate family members and close friends.

❏ 4. If employed, contact the deceased's employer.

❏ 5. If applicable, notify the agent under Power of Attorney.

❏ 6. Alert the executor of your loved one's will.

❏ 7. Notify religious, fraternal, and civic organizations of which your loved one was a member.

❏ 8. Notify your attorney regarding the probate of the estate.

❏ 9. Arrange for the care of any dependents.

❏ 10. If the deceased had any pets, arrange for their immediate care.

❏ 11. Remove any valuables from the deceased's home, secure the residence, and take steps to make the home appear to be occupied (for example, use of lamp timers).

❏ 12. Arrange for the disposal of any perishables left in the deceased's home - such as food, refrigerated items, and existing refuse.

❏ 13. Alert the Post Office to forward the deceased's mail.

❏ 14. Locate loved one's important documents:

> ❏ Will
> ❏ Birth certificate
> ❏ Social Security card
> ❏ Marriage license
> ❏ Military discharge papers (DD-214)
> ❏ Deed to burial property
> ❏ Copy of funeral pre-arrangements
> ❏ Life insurance policies

❏ 15. Compile the following information that the funeral home will need in order to finalize the death certificate:

> ❏ Deceased's first, middle, and last name
> ❏ Deceased's Maiden Name (if applicable)
> ❏ Deceased's Home Address
> ❏ Deceased's Social Security Number
> ❏ Deceased's Date of Birth
> ❏ Deceased's Date of Death
> ❏ Deceased's Age
> ❏ Deceased's Gender
> ❏ Race/Ethnicity
> ❏ Marital Status
> ❏ Spouse's first and last name
> ❏ Deceased's highest level of education attained
> ❏ Deceased's Occupation
> ❏ Deceased's Place of Birth (City and State)
> ❏ Deceased's Father's Name
> ❏ Birth City

❑ Birth State
❑ Deceased's Mother's Name
❑ Birth City
❑ Birth State

If your loved one was a Veteran

❑ Entered Service Date
❑ Entered Service Place
❑ Service Number
❑ Separated from Service Date
❑ Separated from Service Place
❑ Grade, Rank or Rating
❑ Organization and Branch of Service

Within one month of death, you should:

❑ 1. Consult with an attorney about probate.

❑ 2. Meet with an accountant to discuss estate taxes.

❑ 3. File claims with life insurance companies.

❑ 4. Contact the Social Security Administration and other government offices that may have been making payments to the decedent. If the decedent was your spouse, inquire about your eligibility for new benefits.

❑ 5. Notify the Registrar of Voters.

❑ 6. If the deceased's home is unoccupied, cancel unnecessary home services, such as newspaper delivery, cable service, etc.

❑ 7. Cancel the deceased's prescriptions.

❑ 8. Contact the Department of Motor Vehicles to cancel deceased's drivers license and transfer titles of all registered vehicles.

❑ 9. If your loved one was a veteran, inquire about benefits that you may be entitled to through the VA.

❑ 10. Contact the deceased's employer. Inquire about any

401(k), pension, or company benefits that the decedent may be entitled to.

❏ 11. Notify all three credit reporting agencies.

❏ 12. Obtain a current copy of the deceased's credit report.

❏ 13. If the death was accidental, verify whether benefits are available on existing insurance policies.

❏ 14. Check for any life insurance benefits available through existing credit card or loan accounts.

❏ 15. File any outstanding claims for health insurance or Medicare.

❏ 16. Obtain copies of the deceased's outstanding bills.

❏ 17. Locate and/or obtain other important paperwork necessary for the settlement of their estate:

> ❏ At least twelve (12) copies of the certified
>   Death Certificates
> ❏ Real estate deeds and titles
> ❏ Stock certificates
> ❏ Real estate titles
> ❏ Loan paperwork
> ❏ Bank and retirement account statements
> ❏ Last four (4) years of tax returns

❏ 18. Advise all creditors in writing that a death has occurred.

❏ 19. Change ownership of assets and lines of credit.

❏ 20. Update your will.

❏ 21. Update beneficiaries on your life insurance policies, if necessary.

❏ 22. Send acknowledgement cards for flowers, donations, food, kindness. Also remember to thank the pallbearers.

❏ 23. Organize and distribute the decedent's personal belongings.

❏ 24. Remove loved ones from marketing and mailing lists.

<u>IMPORTANT CONTACT INFORMATION</u>

DEPARTMENT OF VETERANS AFFAIRS
1-800-827-1000
www.vba.va.gov/VBA

SOCIAL SECURITY ADMINISTRATION
1-800-772-1213
www.ssa.gov/pgm/links_survivor.htm

CREDIT REPORTING AGENCIES EQUIFAX
1-800-685-1111
www.Equifax.com

TRANSUNION
1-800-888-4213
www.TransUnion.com

EXPERIAN
1-888-397-3742
www.Experian.com

ABOUT THE AUTHOR

Lance Welch is an entrepreneur and speaker as well as a business, personal development & legacy coach. He spent nearly 30 years in corporate America teaching others how to plan for and visualize a better, healthier, more fulfilling future in their business. He has made it his mission to equip, empower, and encourage others to build an intentional legacy.

Lance has been married for over 36 years, has three grown sons and two grandchildren.

www.TheLanceWelch.com

Milton Keynes UK
Ingram Content Group UK Ltd.
UKHW022358070324
438974UK00006B/104/J